EXETER AND THE TRAMS 1882–1931

EXETER AND THE TRAMS 1882–1931

Julia Neville

Exeter Civic Society

First published 2010 by Exeter Civic Society

Designed and typeset by Wordsense Ltd, Edinburgh

Printed and bound by Short-Run Press, Exeter

A catalogue record for this book is available from

the British Library

ISBN 978-0-9544343-1-1

CONTENTS

Foreword

In 2007 John Perkin, the author of *Exeter and Taunton Tramways*, a publication well known to tram enthusiasts, offered Exeter Civic Society on loan his substantial collection of photographs, postcards and other ephemera relating to the trams and tramways of Exeter. His idea was to see the material used in a new publication. The society were delighted to accept the loan, and the challenge, and this book is the product of the research that his suggestion inspired.

Over the past couple of years Peter Caspar, from the society's executive committee, and Julia Neville, together with collaborators from the society itself, from Exeter people and organisations, and from the relatives of some of those who worked on or used the trams, have been preparing this book. The book provides a picture of fifty years in the long life of Exeter, using as its framework the life of the trams, which ran in Exeter between only 1882 and 1931.

Exeter and the Trams, 1882–1931 represents a new departure for the society, whose publications have up to now been focused very much on the built environment of Exeter's streets and spaces. We hope that readers will enjoy our new exercise in history and nostalgia, and will think of a new side of Exeter's history as they travel through its streets.

Margo Swift, Chair,
Exeter Civic Society

Acknowledgements

Exeter Civic Society is first and foremost indebted to John Perkin for his generous loan of the material about the history of Exeter's trams that he has so carefully collected over the years. Many of the photographs in the collection were taken in the late 1920s by Geoffrey Neve Southerden (1905–1943). Geoffrey Southerden was a native Exonian, and the society is pleased to continue the commemoration of this indomitable tram photographer by the republication of some of his images of the last days of the trams.

Peter Caspar oversaw the production of the book on behalf of the society. A number of society members, in particular David Baker, Margaret Batten, David Cornforth, Geoffrey Harding, Hazel Harvey, Dick Passmore, David Snell and Pamela Vaughan, contributed in different ways to its contents. The society has also benefited from the memories and material collected by Exeter people and their descendants: Derek Gent, Bill Hallett, Sylvia Harding, David Hunt, R.J. Michelmore, Margaret Neville, Pat Parker, Frank Potter, Sadru Bhanji, John Trott, Pat Vaughan, Jack Vowler and Denis Ware. Joanna Chisholm at Wordsense brought imagination and an eye for detail to the process of design.

Permission to use material was readily granted by Exeter Memories, Exeter Postcard Society, Alan H. Mazonowicz, the National Tramways Museum, Crich, Seaton Tramway, the South Western Electricity Historical Society and by Devon Library Services. Terry Russell supplied a fresh set of the tram drawings originally supplied to John Perkin and offered comments on the text. The Westcountry Historic Omnibus & Transport Trust opened their archive and offered suggestions. The society is grateful to them all. Every effort was made to trace the specific copyright of the images used and where this has not been possible the society extends its apologies.

EXETER'S
FIRST TRAMS
1882–1905

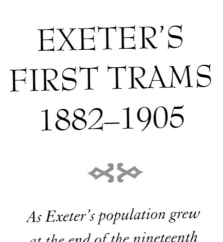

*As Exeter's population grew
at the end of the nineteenth
century, people needed to travel
greater distances to work or
to the city centre. Trams offered
a modern solution.*

Early Victorian Exeter

By the time Queen Victoria came to the throne in 1837, Exeter had reached a state of 'gentle decay'. As Robert Newton, the historian of Exeter's eighteenth and nineteenth centuries described, the city had 'reached and passed the peak of its national importance as a commercial and industrial city'.

The long period of the city's prime, founded on the cloth trade, had been ended by the development of new machines and factories in the Midlands and the North. Mill owners there harnessed the natural resources of fast-flowing rivers to the cheap fuel from local underground coal deposits to produce woollen goods at a much cheaper cost than could be achieved by the old technologies still used in Devon.

By late Georgian times, Exeter was a 'provincial capital',

1 The High Street c.1830, looking in an easterly direction. By this time the city was regarded as being in a state of 'gentle decay'.

a county and diocesan centre, a meeting place for 'good society', a distribution centre and marketplace for agricultural produce from the towns and villages around, and a base for professionals such as solicitors serving the gentry, the farming community and those in trade. All these functions required support and servicing.

2 *Butchers' Row, Smythen Street, The city acted as a market for local produce from the farms around.*

In amongst the older town houses of the gentry and the newer Georgian and Regency terraces like Colleton Crescent and Pennsylvania Buildings (later Pennsylvania Terrace and now Pennsylvania Park), the courts and yards of the city and its immediate suburbs in St Thomas and in Sidwell Street were packed with houses and tenements, homes to the humbler wage-earning population.

3 *This view of Exeter rooftops from the old Conservative Club in Bedford Street at the end of the nineteenth century shows how congested the walled city had become.*

The Coming of the Railways

*I*nside the city the nature of the traffic was very much as it had been in Tudor times. The only wheeled vehicles were handcarts and horse-drawn carts and carriages. The members of the corporation were responsible for the maintenance of the city's streets which, at least in the centre, were paved or cobbled like those in the present Cathedral Close or Stepcote Hill.

The city's centre was also accessible by water, as ships could sail up the Exe and navigate the Exeter Canal up to the quay, where a new basin opened in 1830 offered opportunities for larger vessels to dock. Meanwhile, the old usage of boats and waterways for the transport of goods and passengers had been declining.

By the middle of the eighteenth century, travel into the city by road from the countryside around had improved. Exeter's

4 *Wheeled traffic passing the Guildhall in the mid-nineteenth century was limited to what horses could pull – carts and coaches.*

5 *Stepcote Hill, here in an etching from 1834, is one of Exeter's oldest thoroughfares, with cobbles, a central gutter and steps to climb on either side.*

6 *An 1850s lithograph of the improved arrangements for a basin at the end of the Exeter canal, allowing vessels even of 300 tons to dock and unload.*

Turnpike Trust was established in 1753, and it took responsibility for maintaining the five ways into the city: the London Road, the Bath Road, the Tiverton Road, the Okehampton Road and the Plymouth Road. The age of canals and turnpikes was not to last, however. As part of the great flowering of technological invention and development that took place in the nineteenth century, the arrival of the steam train changed for ever the way in which people thought about distance and travel.

Exeter was not an early beneficiary of railway development.

Bristol and London had been linked by Brunel in 1841, but it was a further three years until, on 1 May 1844, the first Bristol and Exeter Railway train steamed into St David's railway station. The corporation had resisted selling land for a station near the canal basin, and the new station was further up the Exe, about a mile from the city centre. The railway, soon to become the Great Western Railway, continued westwards towards Plymouth with the construction of a viaduct. The new St Thomas railway station was opened in 1846.

7 *The turnpike gate on the Bath Road (shown here) was where the present Pinhoe Road ends at Mount Pleasant Road. This view was taken looking downhill towards the city.*

There had been hopes that the arrival of the new railway would give an impetus to the redevelopment of the economy of Exeter, improving its role as a centre for the distribution of goods. This did not happen immediately, but Exeter's tourist trade did begin to benefit, with the start of excursion trains that made accessible to greater numbers of people what had once been opportunities for the gentry alone.

But progress remained slow. It was not until after the London and South Western Railway arrived in Queen Street in 1861, and Exeter became linked to London through East Devon and Waterloo, as well as via Bristol and Paddington, that the full benefits of the railway came to be realised. As well as the links that the railway brought for Exeter to the big centres of Bristol and London, and across the county to Plymouth and Cornwall, the

8 *An engraving of an early train approaching Great Western Railway's station, now Exeter St David's, made in about 1850.*

development of branch railways was also important for Exeter as a county centre. St David's was linked to Barnstaple in 1854 and along the Exe Valley to Tiverton and Bampton in 1885. Queen Street station was linked to Exmouth in 1862. People from across Devon began to use these new services to travel into Exeter for their shopping or for local events such as the Lammas Fair.

The First Tramway System

Even in the 1930s the old Exeter was still alive in the memories of the older generation. Alderman Lisle, interviewed in the *Express and Echo* on 18 August 1936, remembered: 'The Exeter of my young days [he was born in 1847] was a quiet, almost rural type of place, with green fields where now stretch suburbs with their labyrinth of streets. The St Thomas area was nearly all fields; at

9 *This rural view of Exeter from the Blackboy Road shows that even by the mid-1840s the brick works were producing the materials for the new suburbs.*

Polsloe Park was the mansion of Sir Charles Poltair in a lovely green setting …' By the time Alderman Lisle was born, however, local brickworks were already producing the materials for the building of the new streets.

By the last decades of the nineteenth century more people and goods were indeed coming into Exeter, creating more jobs, needing more people to undertake them. As the opportunities for work in Exeter grew, so did the pressure for housing. The need for homes for so many more people became more than the crowded courts and alleys within the walls could bear, or even the original medieval suburbs of St Sidwell and St Thomas accommodate. Exeter was the site of a building boom that was to continue unchecked for more than half a century.

The old suburb of St Thomas grew by 33 per cent between 1881 and 1891 and 14 per cent between 1891 and 1901. As the gentry moved out to the country from the ring of spaciously set houses on the other bank of the Exe, these fringes of medieval Exeter now provided space for new streets of middle-class and working-class housing. This change occurred first in Newtown, then in Polsloe Park and Mount Pleasant, close to the developing rail yards of the London and South Western Railway line, which provided so much employment.

Streets of new housing also began to join the city to the ring of previously independent settlements and villages outside, with Heavitree the first to become fully linked up. All this meant that more people needed to make longer journeys into and back from the city centre and the railway station. By the time of the 1881 census the population of the city was approaching 50,000. There was an opportunity for an enterprising transport company to meet the needs of this growing population for travel.

In 1881 an Act of Parliament 'for making tramways in the county of Devon to be called Exeter Tramways' was passed. Under this Act the city council agreed running powers over the corporation's streets for the period of twenty-one years. These were assigned to a new commercial company, the Exeter Tramways Company Ltd, whose principal promoters were Messrs Bidder, Buckland and Moore. The Black Horse in Longbrook Street was the base for the company's planning, and it was the landlord there, Mr Collings, who supplied the company with their stables and shed on a site between his premises and New North Road. Final plans were completed at a meeting with shareholders on 15 November 1881, and on 3 January 1882 the construction of the horse-drawn tramways began.

John Trott replied to the Civic Society's appeal for information about the Exeter trams. He lent extracts from the diaries of his grandfather, **William Bidgood**.

William worked at Munk's the ironmonger's in Fore Street (a firm which advertised on the trams) during the early 1880s, and lived with his mother in Sidwell Street. William was interested in the development of the horse-drawn tram system. He noted on 3 January 1882 that they had 'commenced laying the metals for trams in Exeter' and later on, on 8 January, he even 'walked to Heavitree for the purpose of seeing progress', though as he notes it was 'very little'. After that he mentions his first journey by the tramcar on 24 June 1882 'from Bude Hotel to the college' and the time when his aunt went to see his mother and 'returned by tram'. Even in those early days trams did not always run as they were supposed to and William notes problems such as the occasion in January 1883 when his mother waited for a tramcar in the rain for half an hour.

Three lines were established, all radiating from London Inn Square just outside the city's East Gate. The first route ran to St David's station via New North Road, the Obelisk, Hele Road and

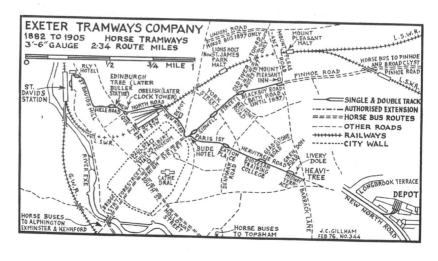

10 *Horse-drawn tram and bus routes, 1882–1905, drawn by J.C. Gillham in 1976.*

St David's Hill; the second to Livery Dole via Paris Street and Heavitree Road; and the third terminated at Mount Pleasant via Sidwell Street and Bath Road. (The obelisk at the end of Queen Street was replaced by the present clock tower in 1897.) The trams were housed in a depot off New North Road (drawn as an inset in the bottom right-hand corner to plate 10, *left*).

On the morning of 6 April 1882, following a Board of Trade inspection, services began on the London Inn Square–Heavitree Road section, leaving from the Bude Hotel and terminating at the Diocesan Training College (later St Luke's). On the following day, Good Friday, a full service of fifty journeys, using two trams, was run between 8.00 a.m. and 10.00 p.m. More than 800 passengers were carried. By 1883 the section along Sidwell Street and up Blackboy Road and the section along New North Road were both in operation.

The original plans had also included a line through the heart of the city from Queen Street and High Street via Bedford Street to the Barnfield, but there was intense opposition to this not just from the High Street and Queen Street traders but also from 'Clergy, Nobility, Gentry and Residents' and the proposal was dropped. A fifth proposed line, a branch from the Obelisk at the New North Road/ Queen Street junction up to the Royal Albert Museum, bringing the passengers in closer to the shopping areas of Queen Street and the High Street, was never constructed. The company did operate a fleet of connecting horse-bus services that would link the tram service to Alphington and Kennford, to Pinhoe and Broadclyst, to Topsham, and to the end of Union Road at the foot of Stoke Hill.

11 *Horse-drawn trams outside the White Lion Hotel in Sidwell Street at the point where the two routes diverged, one to Mount Pleasant and one to Heavitree.*

Problems for the Horse-drawn Trams

Although the Sidwell Street and Heavitree routes became and remained profitable, the failure to gain permission to run the trams along Queen Street and the High Street was a big blow to the company, and made overall financial viability much harder to attain. They were never able to generate the operating surplus that would have enabled them to keep the trams and the tramways in good repair, let alone to extend and improve them. As early as 1883 the company was brought to court for failure to pay interest on its mortgage and to its other creditors. By 1892 the company had been sold to the Tramway Purchase Syndicate, a London company headed by Carritt's, which leased the system on to Frederick Burt and Son to operate.

Trouble continued, though, and in 1893 Sunday services were suspended throughout the spring. The route from St David's to the city centre was (and is) up a steep hill, and the costs of operating it were correspondingly higher than on the other routes. It was first cut back to a Wednesday-only service and then abandoned altogether.

Problems over the maintenance of the track and the surrounding roadway led the city council into further discussions with the company. The company eventually agreed to make the city council a yearly payment towards the maintenance cost of the roadway around the track if the council undertook the work.

The 'Second Industrial Revolution': New Technologies and the Start of 'Commuting'

If the first Industrial Revolution had robbed Exeter of the cloth trade, the second Industrial Revolution, turning new skills and technology to areas such as engineering and electrical work, made a positive difference to employment in Exeter. Henry F. Willey, who ran a successful business making gas meters, and who had been mayor of Exeter in 1872/3, had already moved his works out across the river from Shilhay into St Thomas in 1860, building a new factory where the patent gas meters and other products could be made. His son built houses for some of his workers and leased land to other builders, causing Exeter to stretch out along the west bank of the Exe towards the old village of Alphington. Other firms such as Garton and King the ironmongers also benefited from the new products they were able to make, and so they employed more people.

The corporation pressed for the annexation of the St Thomas district, which would increase the population for which the city took responsibility. This finally came into operation with the passing of the Extension of Boundaries Act 1899. By the census in 1901 the population of Exeter had risen to 59,000. The building and construction trades now employed the greatest number of Exeter men, followed by the hotel and leisure industries, with transport taking third place.

Development of electricity offered a new source of motive power for transport, cleaner and quieter than the coal-fired engines used by railways. Leeds was the first city to introduce electric trams running on roads in 1891, and by 1901 London and other large cities such as Nottingham had begun to install electric tramway systems. Messrs Burt and Co., who were operating the tramways on behalf of the syndicate, raised with the corporation in 1898 the possibility of converting Exeter's tramways to run on electricity and sought their consent to such a development, which then came under active consideration. The corporation agreed in 1899 to the transfer of the tramways undertaking to Burt's from Carritt's, but turned down Burt's suggestion that the corporation should buy him out for £9,300.

1900 – A New Era for the Trams

By the turn of the century the mood of those who owned businesses on Queen Street, Fore Street and the High Street had changed. The benefits that the Sidwell Street traders had experienced from the growing numbers of shoppers brought in by the trams made those who had businesses in other streets keen to have a share in the possible profits to be made.

In the meantime the end of the twenty-one-year life of the Exeter Tramways Act was approaching. In spite of the losses being made on the horse-drawn system, companies were keen to promote the development of electric trams. Two companies, both of which had reached agreement with the Exeter Tramways Syndicate to buy them out, courted the corporation to support their schemes to introduce electric trams. The corporation's experience of its public–private partnership over horse-drawn trams made them reluctant to agree running powers for any outside organisation,

12 *Horse-drawn tram outside 186 Sidwell Street, the premises of James Bealey, paperhanger and decorator.*

and they started to investigate the possibility of running their own scheme. Negotiations came to an end, and even the company that had started to take action to promote a new Parliamentary Bill dropped out.

The timing for the corporation was important. It had the right to purchase the business from Exeter Tramways Company at the end of twenty-one years, but if it failed to do so the original company or its successors automatically had the right to continue to operate. The decision needed to be taken before 1903. The corporation commissioned consultants to report on the feasibility of the operation of a tram service. The Tramways Committee, led by Councillor Perry, went to visit tramway systems in London, Birmingham, Wolverhampton, Bristol, Bournemouth, Southampton and Dover, and even travelled as far as northern France, inspecting trams in Paris, Rouen and Le Havre. The end result of their investigations was the presentation of a report prepared by the city surveyor, Mr Cameron, and its electrical engineer, Mr Munro, which recommended the overhead trolley system. An underground conduit was considered for the High Street and Fore Street, but rejected in favour of uniformity.

In December 1902 the Exeter Tramway Poll, an early version of a referendum, was taken. Ratepayers were asked two questions. The first, 'Do you vote in favour of or against the adoption of the Resolution [for the council to present a Parliamentary Bill to obtain the right to run trams in the city]?' produced 5,187 votes in favour (79 per cent) and 1,384 against. The second question, 'Should the trams run through the High Street?' produced 4,958 votes (75 per

Charles Josiah Ross
Chief Opponent of the Trams

Opposition to the trams by High Street traders was continued by firms such as Hinton Lake the chemists and W.R. Lisle the jewellers. A leading opponent of the introduction of trams to the High Street was C.J. Ross of C. & J. Ross, the draper and outfitter at 227 High Street. Ross was elected to the council in November 1901 for St Petrock's Ward and pledged to oppose the plans. He was part of the 1902 fact-finding mission to other towns where electric trams already ran.

Together with G.F. Gratwicke he is pictured in a hostile cartoon of the period under the heading of 'Trams, Taxes and Tarraddidles!', frightening the citizens of Exeter with 'The Bogey Man', their claim that the cost of the trams was unaffordable.

13 *Supporters of electric trams produced a handbill with a cartoon of Ross and Gratwicke and their 'Bogeyman', representing their wild estimates of costs. Ratepayers were urged to vote in support of 'Tramways for Exeter'.*

Those in favour of the trams claimed that Ross and Gratwicke, 'the anti-Tramites' wanted 'to control, in the supposed interest of their customers, the main street of Exeter'. But 'the High Street belongs to Exonians generally', the pro-tram lobby pointed out, 'and not merely to the Tradesmen in that street and their patrons'.

Charles Ross lost the battle over the introduction of the electric trams to the High Street, but he remained an implacable opponent of the trams and lost no opportunity to speak out against the problems he claimed they caused.

cent) in favour and 1,621 against. The resounding victory gave the council, which had been elected that November, a robust mandate to develop an electric tram system for the city.

Early in 1903, on 27 February, the 'Great Tramway Meeting' as the *Devon Evening Express* called it, took place, offering supporters a final chance to declare for the proposal for the electric tramway system. An old Exonian, a former mayor of Southampton, had been invited back to his native city to press the case for the electric trams that Southampton had already adopted. The meeting was chaired by H.A. Willey who, as a 'plain business man', enthusiastically put the business case for the electric trams, reminding his hearers that twenty out of forty county towns had

14 *The growing demand for electric power and light at the end of the nineteenth century led the corporation to invest in a new electricity generating station at Haven Banks.*

now installed tramways systems. He dismissed the opposition, referring to 'a certain section of citizens whose timidity suggests that the institution of tramways into the city and their passage through the main thoroughfares will injure them' and stressing that the profits would be sufficient to produce a reduction in the rates.

Willey pointed out that one of the benefits of electrification would be to provide a 'day load' for the newly municipalised City of Exeter Electricity Company, to complement the load the company dealt with during the hours of darkness. The original Exeter Electric Light Company had been formed at the end of the 1880s, but, like the trams, struggled to make enough of a profit to fund the investment necessary to keep pace with the developing technology. By 1896 the corporation had bought out the company, and the City of Exeter Electricity Company undertook the operation from then on. By 1899 the corporation were actively looking for a new site to replace the original one on New North Road, and by 1904 new premises had been built at Haven Banks on the west bank of the Exe. New business was being actively sought.

The 'stirring and enthusiastic meeting' solidly supported the proposal for an electric tram system, and thus in the parliamentary session of 1903 a Bill was presented to secure for the corporation the right to buy out the Exeter Tramways Company and to construct new tramways for the city. Although opposed in Parliament, the Bill was finally passed. Councillor Perry, Tramways Committee chairman, and his colleagues were now responsible for implementing the new system and operating the tramways service.

This was not a cheap scheme, even though it was described by Willey at the 'Great Tramways Meeting' as one where the capital required was 'moderate in the extreme'. The cost to the corporation of setting it up was more than fifty thousand pounds at 1903 prices, representing an expenditure in modern terms of more than five million pounds. In addition, the corporation had to purchase the buildings, stock, track and horses of the Exeter Tramways Company enterprise. The cost was made up as follows:

COST TO THE CITY COUNCIL OF SETTING UP THE ELECTRIC TRAMWAYS

Infrastructure	£
New track and wooden paving	34,000
Overhead equipment	4,700
Feed cables	3,000
Tramcars	7,000
Depot	5,700
Generating plant	4,000
Cost of purchasing the Exeter Tramways undertaking	6,800
Total	**65,2000**

Setting up the new system involved immense disruption
to the everyday life of the High Street. In 1904 the local press
reported that:

> The High Street is just now in its throes. From London Inn Square to
> Queen Street ... between the end of Queen Street and Broadgate, two-
> thirds of the width is under the disturbing influence of the excavator ...
> Below Broadgate the three properties immediately next to the new bank
> buildings (the Maypole Dairy, Gimblett's and the Tofferies) are in course
> of demolition preparatory to the laying down of the new street line, and
> Messrs Holman, Ham and Company's large premises at the corner of
> South Street are in the hands of contractors for setting back.

It is from this time that the western end of the High Street took
on its now familiar look, with St Petrock's Church, which had been
hidden for centuries, reappearing on the street frontage. Under
protest the rector and the church wardens exchanged the land on
which the church porch stood for part of an adjacent site.

15 *The laying of
the new track for
the trams must have
caused immense
disruption in the
High Street as the
photo here of the
Queen Street
corner shows.*

1905 – Inauguration of the First Electric Trams

*T*he electric trams were given a working trial on the night of 24 March 1905, with a run from the new depot at the bottom of Paris Street (see p.49). The first car, bearing an illuminated sign, 'Special', at either end, set off up the hill to Livery Dole. Some hearts must have missed a beat when, as the tram turned from the depot into the main street, all its lights went out, but this was a minor technical problem with the engagement of the trolley arm, and soon put to rights. The Board of Trade inspector approved the new system for operation from 3 April.

16 *Crowds thronged the High Street for the inauguration of the electric tram service on 4 April 1905. Note the only horse-drawn tram ever to travel down the High Street.*

The official opening was planned for 4 April 1905. At 12.30 p.m. five trams were lined up at the Guildhall. The mayor, Councillor E. Perry, was given the honour of driving the tram up the High Street to London Inn Square down Paris Street and up the Heavitree Road to Livery Dole. Once the tram had returned to the Guildhall the mayor addressed the crowd from the top deck of the first tram. He reminded the crowds of the 'twenty-two years of inefficient service' they had endured

from the horse-drawn trams, and
'trusted they would see no more of
them'. To mark the occasion the
mayoress was given a bouquet of
carnations and white heather from
which hung a horseshoe taken
from one of the tramway horses.
A silver tram handle, now in the
Exeter Guildhall collection, was
given by the consulting engineer
to Perry himself.

For most people the introduction
of the electric trams was an excitement, a novelty and then a very
useful service, as shown in a postcard sent on 20 April, a fortnight
after the new service had begun (see plate 19, p.32). Those who

*17 The mayor,
Councillor E. Perry,
who also chaired
the Tramways
Committee, was
given the honour
of driving the first
tram, suitably decked
out with flowers
and flags.*

*18 From the top
deck of the tram, the
mayor made a speech
celebrating the new
municipal service, the
Exeter Corporation
Tramways.*

had enjoyed the horse-drawn tram, however, mourned the end of an era in the traditional style still current in the Edwardian era, with the production of a 'mourning card' (see plate 20, *below*).

19 *A postcard sent by an Exonian remarked on the introduction of 'our new trams' and the difference between the old and the new.*

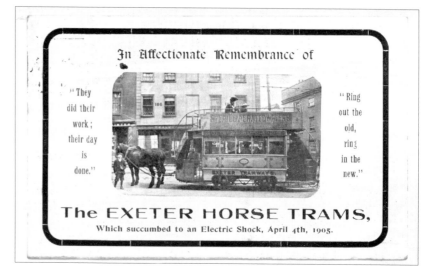

20 *'Mourning cards' were the way in which Edwardian society commemorated a death. This card 'mourns' the passing of the horse-drawn trams.*

CABS, HORSES
AND CARS

*Exeter's trams were
double-deckers almost from the
beginning. Downstairs passengers
travelled cosily inside the car;
upstairs they were exposed to the
worst of the weather.*

The Horse-drawn Tramcars

The first 'tramcars' evolved from coaches and wagons. The majority of Exeter's horse-drawn trams, and all the electric trams, were open-top double-deckers, as the old post chaises had been. They carried passengers both inside, away from the worst of the weather, and also on top, where there was no overhead protection at all. A particular feature of all tramcars, whether horse-drawn or powered by electricity, was that as they ran on rails they had to be double-ended if the operators were to avoid the considerable expenditure of providing turntables at each route terminus. At each end of a tramcar, therefore, there was a broad platform. On twin-crewed trams, as those in Exeter always were, these were used from the front by the driver to operate the car and from the rear by the passengers, for getting on and off. The platform at whichever was the leading end in use on the car was closed off from the street and the dangers of other traffic by a rope or a folding gate to prevent passengers from boarding at the front.

When the tram reached the end of its journey the driver changed ends,

21 The reverse silver-plated tram handle presented to H.E. Bradley, chairman of the Transport Committee, commemorating Exeter Corporation Tramways, 1905–1931, on 19 August 1931. The tram handle is now in the Exeter Guildhall collection.

leaving what was now the rear platform open and pulling the fastening across the front platform. On a horse-drawn car the horses were unharnessed and taken round to the 'new' front end. On the electric cars the motorman unlocked and took to the other end the 'handle', the device locked into the control panel through which the motorman controlled the amount of power to be applied to the motors.

No pictures have yet been traced of the very first Exeter horse-drawn cars, which were single deckers. Three were bought for the initial opening in 1882; three more once all the routes came into service on 1 August 1883; and two more the year after. All Exeter Tramways Company cars were painted yellow, with chocolate-brown lettering. They were built by Bristol Wagon and Carriage Works Company, and seated sixteen passengers, twelve inside and four more on the rear platform. The *Flying Post* reassured passengers about their safety: 'Very powerful brakes are fitted in such a way as to be under the complete control of the driver and conductor, either of whom will be able, with one turn of the brake-handle, to pull up the car within half its length.' Nonetheless accidents did occur. The worst horse-tram accident took place on 26 September 1885, when the brakes failed on a car descending St David's Hill and the car overturned. Four passengers and the horses were injured.

At a later date, probably during the mid-1890s, the company changed over to four-wheel double-deck open-top cars, again manufactured by Bristol Wagon and Carriage Works. They bought at least six of these before they sold the business to Exeter Corporation, two in 1896 and at least one in 1900. These are the cars featured in the surviving photographs (see, for example, plate 22, *below*). Their four arched windows appear to have curtains inside them, and some kind of stickers or advertisements on the glass. Possibly these were prohibitory notices, requiring passengers to refrain from spitting or smoking.

22 (above)
A horse-drawn tram on Heavitree Road. The livery used by the Exeter Tramways Company was yellow with chocolate-brown lettering.

23 (right) *'Toast-rack'-style car, originally from the Isle of Man, now in the Seaton Tramway collection.*

It also appears that, although the company had switched to double-deckers, they did buy one last single-deck tram in what was known as the 'toast-rack' design. An example of this type of car is shown in plate 23 (*bottom left*), which, originally from the Isle of Man, now forms part of the Seaton Tramway collection.

When in 1904 the corporation came to buy the stock, at a price fixed at arbitration of £6,749, there were four double-deckers and one single-decker left in service. A year later these five cars, together with the harnesses, made £51 for the corporation at the auction run by Messrs Reed and Goss.

The Horses

Each car was pulled by a pair of horses, and farmers around Exeter were able to make a bit of extra income by breaking-in horses for the Tramways Company. The young colts would be led up to the farms through the streets of the city and spend time learning to pull carts safely before they went on to pull the trams. Eventually, at the other end of their careers, horses that were no longer up to pulling the cars were sold back to the farmers at a lower price than they had reached when in their prime, and they returned to lighter duties on the farm.

The tramway horses, which were stabled at the depot in New North Road, were reputed not to have been well cared-for by the company. Several of the tramcar drivers were in fact convicted of cruelty to their horses, and fined by amounts ranging from 5s. (25p) to 40s. (£2). In 1895 a repeat offender was even given a prison sentence of one month.

In 1905 when the switch-over of tram power from horse to electricity occurred, the last remaining twenty-two horses were auctioned off by Collings' for about £15 each. The corporation received £263 11*s*. 6*d*. in total. Most unfortunately, one of the horses reared, fell and died from its injuries only 200 yards away from the auctioneer's stables. The purchaser, W.H. Copp, applied to the corporation for redress. The corporation agreed to reimburse him half his money back – £8 18*s*. 6*d*. instead of the seventeen guineas he had paid.

The Electric Tramcars

24 Car no. 4 towards the end of its working life, ready to pick up passengers in Heavitree for the city centre and Dunsford Road.

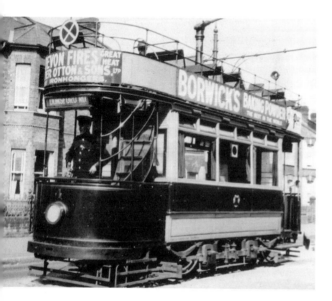

In all, over the twenty-six years of operation Exeter Corporation Tramways purchased thirty-seven tramcars, numbered 1 to 34 (omitting number 13), and 1 to 4 (second series). All the cars had a four-wheel base and all had open upper decks. The Board of Trade had reservations about four-wheel covered-top cars on narrow-gauge tramways, as such cars were considered to be less stable in high winds and to be more prone to accidents than cars running on eight wheels or on broader gauges. The schedules (*opposite* and on p.40) are based on information collated by R.C. Sambourne.

SCHEDULE OF ELECTRIC TRAMS PURCHASED BY EXETER CORPORATION TRAMWAYS, 1905–1931, ORIGINAL NUMBERING

Car	Date of Purchase	Body	Truck	Electrical Equipment	Seats
1	April 1905	Dick, Kerr	Brill 21E, 5ft 6in	Dick, Kerr 2 × 25hp motors	42
2					
3					
4					
5					
6					
7					
8					
9					
10					
11					
12					
14	Sept 1905	Dick, Kerr	Brill 21E, 5ft 6in	Dick, Kerr 2 × 25hp motors	42
15					
16	Aug 1906	Dick, Kerr	Brill 21E, 5ft 6in	Dick, Kerr 2 × 25hp motors	42
17					
18					
19					
20					
21					
22	Dec 1914	Brush	Brill 21E, 5ft 6in	Dick, Kerr 2 × 34hp motors	44
23					
24					
25					
26	Nov 1921	Brush	Peckham P22, 7ft 6in	Dick, Kerr 2 × 35hp motors	54
27					
28	Sept 1925	Brush	Brill 21E, 7ft 0in	British Thompson Houston 2 × 40hp motors	54
29					
30					
31	May 1926				
32					
33					
34					

SCHEDULE OF ELECTRIC TRAMS PURCHASED BY EXETER CORPORATION TRAMWAYS, 1905–1931, NEW NUMBERING

Car		Body	Truck	Electrical Equipment	Seats
1	Mar 1929	Brush	Peckham P35, 7ft 6in	General Elec. Co, 2 × 50 hp motors	53
2	Ordered for				
3	Whipton				
4	extension which was never constructed				

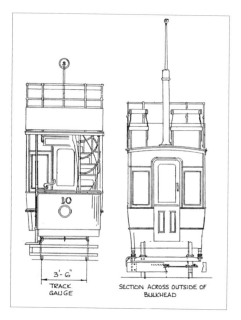

Figure 1 *Sections of an early electric tramcar showing the internal staircase (left) and across the bulkhead (right) (drawn by Terry Russell).*

TRACK GAUGE 3'-6"

SECTION ACROSS OUTSIDE OF BULKHEAD

The first electric cars, nos 1 to 12, were bought for the opening of the service in 1905, and seated twenty on the lower deck (the saloon) and twenty-two on the upper deck. Their acquisition was (after passenger journeys exceeded expectations) almost immediately followed by the purchase of cars nos 14 and 15 at a price each that was £10 dearer than that paid for the first batch. This allowed for the extension of the initial short running of the routes to the full approved length. The number 13, presumably for superstitious reasons, was never used for any car in the fleet. Plate 24 (see p.38) shows car no. 4 of the first series, though not in the earliest livery, which would have had the wording 'Exeter Corporation Tramways' on the side boards. The characteristics that mark out this tram as an early one are the simple two-level safety rail fencing on the upper deck, the overhead lights on the upper deck (shown most clearly at the far end), the unenclosed area in front of the driver, and the destination board suspended above the driver, in this case showing 'Dunsford Road'. All these cars, and those that followed, up to the First World War, were built for Messrs Dick, Kerr and Co. of Preston. The maintenance wagon, on the other hand, which cost almost £68, was built by Messrs S. Rawlinson and Sons of Blackburn. The layout and external appearance of the first twenty-one cars is shown in figures 1 (*left*) and 2 (*below*). The scale is 7mm to 1ft.

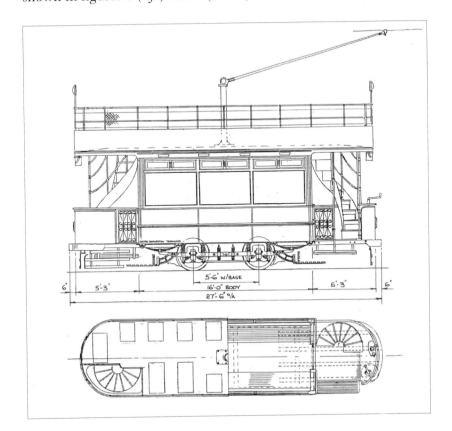

Figure 2 *Layout and external view of an early electric tramcar (drawn by Terry Russell. Note the lattice gates with which the motorman could close off the platform at the driver's end.*

25 Car no. 20 stationary at the Heavitree terminus (Cross Park).

26 Car no.17 outside the Great Western Hotel, about to turn up St David's Hill. The paintwork was dark green and cream, with gold lettering highlighted in pink.

For the opening in 1906 of the next phase of the system, across the new Exe Bridge both to the top of Cowick Street and out to the Alphington Road, car nos 16 to 21 were acquired. They were built to an almost identical model, although in fact they had slightly higher guard rails. Car no. 20 is from this batch (see plate 25, *above*). On car no. 17, the old livery was still *in situ* with 'Exeter Corporation Tramways' proudly displayed on the side boards (see plate 26, *left*). Unfortunately a monochrome photograph cannot show the gold lettering, picked out with

pink shading. The main coachwork of the electric tramcars was always dark green and cream, and the undercarriage was painted in dark maroon.

The destination boards with the names of the terminuses were supplemented from 1907 onwards by the display of visual symbols, rather than by letters or numbers later used on the buses, to denote the routes. This could have been an attempt to address the needs of the relatively large proportion of the population who, at least in the early Edwardian days when the trams came into service, might have been illiterate. These symbols were displayed in the side window of the tram as well as at the front and the rear. The Heavitree to Dunsford Road line was marked with a white saltire cross on a red ground (seen in plate 25, *top left*); the Pinhoe Road to Alphington Road line with a green circle on a white ground (seen in plate 30, p.46); and the Queen Street to St David's spur with a white circle on a green ground (seen on the first tram in plate 33, p.47).

At a later date, the guard rails round the top deck were filled in with mesh (see plate 27, *right*, of car no. 19). This tram has been refitted by the in-house maintenance team, with the destination board now raised on to the railings of the upper deck and with angular windscreens introduced at the front to make an enclosed vestibule. The top light opened

27 *The sign for the Queen Street to St David's route, a white circle on a green ground, is clearly shown on car no. 19, here heading up to Queen Street.*

28 *Car no. 24, taken at Livery Dole on the Heavitree route, was part of the group bought just before the First World War.*

to provide some ventilation and to allow the driver to see better when it was raining as there were no windscreen wipers.

The final pre-war purchases, similar in design and also built for Dick, Kerr and Co., were the three cars, nos 22 to 25, bought in 1914 at a cost of £708 each. This was not the lowest tender for the new cars but was accepted by the corporation to secure compatibility with existing rolling stock. Plate 28 (*left*) shows one of these trams, which was of a design almost identical to that used for cars nos 16 to 21, with motorman Gil Easterbrooke and his conductor standing beside it. Motormen and their conductors worked for years in regular pairings.

Inside the cars, the seats were set out in two rows facing each other, sideways to the direction of travel (see plate 29, *right*). The corporation bye-laws included one allowing the conductor to stop someone from using a tram if it was considered their clothing would soil the cushions or indeed the clothes other passengers were wearing. The first 'cushions' were made of rattan (wicker), and mats made for the floors were purchased from the Institution for the Blind. The garden-type double seats on the top deck had reversible backs (see plate 53, p.70). It was the responsibility of the conductor at the terminus to go upstairs and make sure the seats were facing in the correct direction for the return journey. Of course, passengers in groups took the opportunity to move the seat backs for themselves and sit in groups to chat. The seats were regularly rained on, and the corporation went to considerable trouble to find an appropriate fabric in which to cover them.

In 1921, as a result of the extra wear and tear caused by the problems with track and car maintenance during the First World War, the corporation bought two new cars, no. 26 (see plate 68, p.88) and no. 27. Car no. 27 was modified in 1926 (see plate 30, p.46), with new angular dashes, platform vestibule and blind. Note the way in which the destination symbol now appears to house a light to show up the route symbol in the dark. The destination board was now routinely provided in an upper position instead of suspended above the driver.

The new arrangement also helped with another problem – rain, cold and wind affecting the drivers. In 1905 the first waterproof coats purchased were found to be inadequate and the committee was compelled to investigate the purchase of oilskins. They also bought the drivers some gloves. The new design of the cab with windscreens to the side also gave the drivers more protection from

29 Inside a tram car in 1929. The conductor collects the fares. Note the ornate shades over the electric lamps.

the weather, although the enclosed cab does not appear to have had any windscreen wipers. The top light opened, presumably with the aim of throwing off the rain to either side of the main window.

Cars nos 26 and 27, and all those purchased by the corporation from no.22

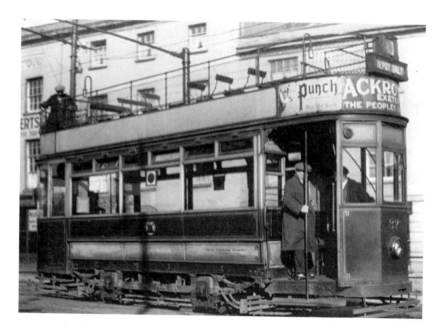

30 *Car no. 27, purchased in 1921, standing outside the tram depot at the foot of Paris Street.*

onwards, were built by Messrs Brush and Co. as Dick, Kerr and Co. had stopped supplying carriages to concentrate on electrical equipment. They were longer than the first trams, with wheelbases measuring 7ft rather than 5ft 6in, and seated twenty-four rather than twenty-two on the top deck. Cars nos 28 to 30 were bought almost four years later, in 1925, and were the first to be delivered with an integrated platform vestibule (see plate 70, p.89, of car no. 28). These Brush cars were followed by the final cars in the first series, nos 31 to 34, purchased in 1926 and virtually identical (see plate 32, *right centre*). Plate 33 (*right bottom*) shows car nos 4 and 32, offering a contrast between the older Dick, Kerr series and the newer Brush models.

31 (right) *The stripped body of a car sits in the depot. The notice inside the vestibule advertises the bus service to Pennsylvania.*

32 (above) *Car no. 30, waiting outside the depot at the foot of Paris Street. Note the sign with a green circle on a white ground for the Alphington Road route.*

33 (right) *The old and the new: car nos 4 and 32 waiting at Belmont Road, 17 September 1927.*

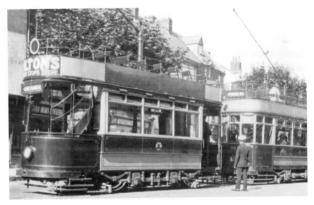

34 New car no. 2, part of the final batch of trams delivered in 1929.

35 The original car no. 7 inside the workshop at the tram depot, preparing for a new life as a snow plough.

By the end of the 1920s the final days of the trams were approaching. The Tramways Committee received permission for what were to be the last four cars, nos 1 to 4 (second series), illustrated here in plate 34 (*above*) of car no. 2 of the second series. These last cars, fitted with Peckham P35 trucks, were delivered in 1929, only months before the decision to close the tramways was made. They replaced the original cars nos 1, 5, 17 and 21. The original car nos 2, 3 and 4 were renumbered as 5, 7 and 19 and went back into service. The original car no. 7 was modified and ended its life as a snow plough. Plate 35 (*left*) shows it undergoing work in the depot.

36 *The façade of the electric tram depot as it appeared long after the trams had gone. The roller-shutter doors conceal the fact that there were four bays rather than two, shown by the brick arches above.*

The Depot

37 *The tram depot, shown here on the map drawn by J.C. Gillham, was located at the foot of Paris Street, which in the tram era led directly into the Heavitree Road.*

The old depot for the horse-drawn trams was in New North Road. The tram shed and stables, which were owned by the landlord of the Black Horse in Longbrook Street, were situated on the site between the Old Fire House and Locomotive Inns. The new depot for the electric trams was built at what was then the foot of Paris Street (see plate 36, *above*), adjacent to the site where the swimming baths (2009 Pyramid Swimming Baths) were constructed in the 1930s. Plate 37 (*below*) shows the detail of the layout backing on to Athelstan Road.

After the tram fleet was sold off, the depot was used as a bus garage

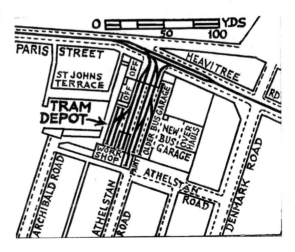

until the building of the Paris Street bus station. Plate 96 (p.123) shows the building awaiting demolition. In its heyday it was smartly kept, with troughs of plants between each of the open archways. Inside the shed (see plate 38, *below*), the four access tracks had inspection pits beneath the rails, and there was also a short bay to allow for the movement of trams within the shed.

38 The interior of the tram depot was designed so that trams could be moved over inspection pits when repairs were necessary. After the First World War a rear extension was built for additional workshops.

THE HEYDAY OF THE TRAMS

The trams made it easier for people to come into the centre of the city, and opportunities for shopping and for leisure activities increased to meet the new demand.

Trams West of the Exe

The first services, run by the first twelve trams, operated from the Guildhall to the Mount Pleasant Inn, and from St David's to Livery Dole. These covered less than two-thirds of the routes the Tramways Committee had planned. By 29 April 1905, however, Board of Trade approval had been given to the first major extension, taking the services out into Heavitree and over the new Exe Bridge to Cowick Street up to Dunsford Gate at the junction with Buddle Lane.

Over the previous two years the major task of replacing the Georgian Exe Bridge had been under way. The original bridge was dismantled and a temporary, pontoon, structure put in place. On 23 July 1904 the mayor (F.J. Widgery) had laid the foundation stone for the new structure that supported a wider, more level

39 *Exe Bridge from the St Thomas side, taken in the early days of the trams. All other wheeled traffic is horse-drawn.*

40 *On 29 September 1906 Mayor Tom Linscott opened the Alphington Road section of the tram service. Here he is pictured driving car no. 21, one of the corporation's newest trams.*

bridge of modern steel construction. The bridge itself was opened on 29 March 1905, just before the electric tram service began.

The construction work to extend the tramway service to its full length, by taking it along the Alphington Road, then absorbed a further eighteen months. By September 1906 all was in place. On 29 September the mayor, Tom Linscott, drove the first tram along the new route down to Stone Lane, Alphington with the support of crowds just as extensive as those that had lined the streets in the city centre the previous year.

The electric trams were immediately popular. By June 1905, before the opening of the Alphington extension, the average numbers of passengers was up to 80,000 per week. The committee was almost embarrassed by the numbers using the trams in the first few weeks and struggled to keep the services going according to the planned timetable, with too few trained motormen and only twelve trams.

41 An Edwardian view of Queen Street from the High Street with the Higher Market on the left. This was seen as an appropriate topic for a Christmas card!

Trams and the Everyday Life of the City

*I*t is difficult to imagine what impact the arrival of the electric trams had on a city where travel and the movement of goods for sale and delivery were still almost entirely dependent on the horse. Early photographs of the electric trams show bicycles and carts or wagons pulled by horses as the only other wheeled traffic on the streets.

The tram service had some unexpected consequences for other traffic. The chapter clerk wrote to the corporation in September 1905 complaining about the disruptive impact of the increased traffic between Broadgate and Palace Gate since the introduction of the trams. Presumably it was being used as a shortcut to avoid the busy sections approaching the High Street/Fore Street junction.

People in the early twentieth century usually walked to work and back, but the growth of Exeter's suburbs meant that this became increasingly difficult and time-consuming. It is probably no coincidence that H.A. Willey of Willey's Foundry was a great supporter of the extension and improvement of the tramways system as the firm, based down at Haven Banks, was a major Exeter employer and needed to draw on a wide pool of labour. The needs of the commuters were met by the development of a special fare structure for 'workers'. This offered cheaper fares, rather than the modern more expensive 'peak' fares, for early morning and early evening travel. On Saturdays, when most people still worked a half-day during the morning, the cheap return fare applied in the early afternoon rather than the evening.

One of the worries about the ultimate replacement of the trams was whether buses would be able to cope with the load the trams took in the lunch hour as commuters followed the then common practice of returning home for a midday meal and travelling back to work. School children also used the trams for regular journeys to school and also for opportunities such as the trips to the swimming baths for lessons.

Before the widespread use of the wireless for mass communication the centre of the city was the place for public announcements, such as the death of the king or

42 The crowd catching their trams at this stop on Sidwell Street includes a number of school age children. Many of the buildings seen in the postcard are still in place today.

the crying of the Lammas Fair. People from outer areas of the city came in to find out what was going on. The *Express and Echo* set up its High Street premises, at that time close to the Queen Street corner, for the night of the General Election on 30 October 1924, with a system of blue, green and red electric light bulbs to flash on as the news of a Conservative, a Liberal or a Labour victory was declared. This proved so popular that the throng of people waiting for the results to be declared was too great at one point for the trams to be able to pass down the High Street.

Exeter retained its role as a major centre not only for its own population but also for a wide hinterland around it, now linked by the train as well as by horse-drawn transport. The trams were used by city residents as well as those who came in from the villages outside to the railway stations. One such trip on 5 June 1923 proved fatal for the rector of Bickleigh. The Rev. Walter Carew had come into St David's station by train with a group of friends from

43 *As the city grew the trams were an important link from the growing suburbs into the town centre. Here a tram is descending the hill into Heavitree.*

Bickleigh and the Exe Valley
in order to attend the Diocesan
Conference at the Civic Hall.
He boarded a tram at the station
and took a seat on the upper
deck, but by the time the tram
had reached Hele Road his
friends called the conductor
to say he had collapsed. In

44 Catching the tram at St David's station was a popular way of travelling up the steep hill to the city centre for people coming in from the surrounding villages.

fact he had died. The tram crew decided to go ahead towards the
Dispensary in Queen Street for medical aid, but as they passed
two policemen on the way they decided to call on them instead.
The St John Ambulance motor was summoned, and it took him
to the mortuary.

The early twentieth century saw some changes in the style of
shopping, particularly with the development of department stores
such as Colson's (now the House of Fraser), Green's (later Bobbys
and the predecessor of Debenham's) and Walton's (on the Queen
Street/High Street corner). The Sidwell Street/High Street/Fore
Street stretch carried some shops and services that have survived
through many changes, such as Boots or Marks and Spencer. In
the heyday of the trams, Exeter also offered a greater range of shops
selling goods that would now tend to be found in specialist or out-
of-town centres, such as Havill's (the butcher with a Macfisheries
counter), Munks the ironmongers, Walter Otton the builder's
merchant or Guest's Pianos.

Shopping started to become a focus for leisure time too, with

45 *Shops changed in the age of the trams. Establishments like the Swiss Café offered shoppers the opportunity for a cup of tea or coffee while they rested their feet.*

the ease of travel allowing shoppers to pause for morning coffee or afternoon tea at centres like Depaoli's Swiss Café (see plate 45, *above*). Alternatively, they could go to department stores like Walton's, which had blazed the trail by opening a tea room in 1913, or Colson's, for the 'dainty teas' their advertisements on the front of the trams promoted.

Earning Extra Revenue for the Tramways

Advertising on the backs of tickets was accepted from the start of the service by Exeter Corporation Tramways. In 1905 W. Bruford and Son, the High Street jewellers, won the first corporation contract to advertise on the backs of the first million tickets. Whether or not the trams should carry advertisements on their coachwork was a topic which greatly exercised the Tramways

46 *By the end of their life all electric trams carried advertisements, sometimes national, sometimes for local establishments like Colson's or the Cathedral Dairy.*

Committee throughout the life of the trams.

The old horse-drawn trams had always carried advertisements on their coachwork (see plate 22, p.36). But once the trams were owned by the city, the committee had to

take a view on whether advertising was compatible with the dignity of a civic service. It would, as one alderman commented, 'vulgarise the whole appearance of the streets of the city'. The topic was discussed before the service began, in 1903, and again in 1906/7 and was permitted on a temporary basis for St Sidwell's

47 *This photograph of a horse-drawn tram in Heavitree shows an advertisement for the national brand of Fry's Cocoa.*

48 The Organising Committee and the Exonian Military Band pose for a photograph on a tram during St Sidwell's Shopping Week.

shopping week, October 1910. Early cards showing advertisements were sometimes produced purely for advertisement and had been 'mocked up' (see plate 49, *top right*). Advertisements were discussed again after the war, in May 1920, when a London firm offered £30 per car per year to place enamelled plate advertisements on the 'decency boards' that encased the top deck and coloured glass advertisements on the ventilators. Some members were for it, but others remained concerned that it was inappropriate for a corporation service.

Charles Ross, now an Alderman, who had developed no enthusiasm for the trams since he opposed them at the start of the century, felt that it was inconsistent to disapprove of the advertisements when they allowed 'hideous railways', i.e. the trams, to run up and down 'one of the most ancient and delightful streets in England'.

The decision this time came down in favour of advertising, which would earn approximately £550 per year. Two years later, Alderman F.J. Widgery, who was an artist by profession, complained about 'the lack of harmony of colour tone' in the advertisements. His aesthetic protest

(though he assured the council he was not 'a crank') was robustly supported by Councillor Tarr, who said the colours of some of the advertisements 'were enough to give people the bile to look at'.

49 Promotional postcard of Exeter's first tram with 'mock-up' advertisements for Green & Son, the High Street costumier, milliner and ladies' and children's outfitter.

50 Shopping at the upper end of the High Street, with the entrance to the Arcade, destroyed in the blitz in 1942, on the left-hand side.

The city was so proud of the trams that the mayor and corporation used them *en masse* on special occasions such as for travelling to the County Show in the fields at Whipton in Show Week, a big event that generated a lot of tram traffic. In 1909 the council – 'all except Alderman Ross, who walked' – went by tram as far as the terminus.

The stately nature of the civic enterprise must have been rather spoilt by the need to display large notices in the car windows facing outwards and reading 'Beware of Pickpockets'. The bye-laws or regulations show something about the behaviour of a minority of passengers – and what the majority considered important. The bye-laws prohibited smoking inside the trams (those wishing to smoke travelled on the top deck); spitting (a rule that had originated in the desire to avoid this possible source of TB infection); playing musical instruments; and carrying loaded firearms, dangerous implements or even dogs. Passengers were forbidden to use offensive language, and various safety measures were put in place, such as prohibiting mounting or dismounting at the front (driver's) end. Passengers were also asked not to tip the crew, although occasionally at Christmas time collecting boxes would be placed in the cars. As one passenger wrote in 1910: 'The drivers and conductors are so civil that they deserve some recognition just as postmen and others.'

Fare-dodging was a continuing problem. After several episodes during the First World War when soldiers in uniform attempted to avoid paying the fare back to the barracks on a Saturday night and 'threatened the conductors as to what they would do', the

town clerk complained in 1915 to the commanding officer at
the barracks about the 'disorderly conduct' of the soldiers. The
adjutant responded promptly that he had 'taken such steps as
will, I hope, make the recurrence of such discreditable behaviour
impossible'. The bye-laws were subsequently revised to include
the more stringent requirement that:

> Every passenger shall before leaving the car pay to the conductor the
> fare legally payable for his journey and accept a ticket therefore. Such
> tickets shall not be transferable and shall be available only for the
> journey and on the car for and on which the same is issued, except
> in the case of special return tickets. Any person leaving a car shall be
> deemed to have completed his journey.

Leisure and Entertainment

The first half of the twentieth century was a peak period for the use
of sites in central locations for organised leisure. Organised football
drew crowds to see the Exeter team, the Grecians, play at St James's
Park. Trams would wait to
take the departing crowds on
their homeward journeys. A
special siding was added to the
track at Belmont Road for this
purpose. At the other end of
town, trams would also wait
for the crowds at Stone Lane
on the Alphington Road close

51 *Trams waiting
at Belmont Road to
collect the crowds
returning from the
football match at
St James's Park.*

to the County Ground at Church Road, St Thomas, which was used for rugby, greyhound racing and, for a couple of years from 1929, speedway. It was also popular for more general events such as festivities to celebrate coronations.

Although then as now there was no major exhibition centre in the middle of the city, the Civic Hall had been opened in the 1920s in the Higher Market in Queen Street to replace the earlier Victoria Hall. This was the place where events such as the West Country Exhibition and the Devon and Exeter Horticultural Society Autumn Show took place. The Drill Hall in Bedford Street was the venue for exhibitions by groups such as the Devon Federation of Master Bakers, while the Barnfield Hall hosted events such as the Exeter Chamber Music Club's Schubert Centenary Concert or the Church Missionary Society's Annual Meeting. There were Sunday services, with visiting preachers well advertised, and free Saturday lectures given by staff of the University College. In 1928 these included 'The League of Nations and the Next War', 'Whales' (with lantern slides) and 'The Exeter Freak Primrose'.

In the centre of town there was live theatre at the Hippodrome in London Inn Square and at the Theatre Royal on Longbrook Street, playing in October 1930, for example, *Rose Marie*, 'the phenomenal Drury Lane success', followed by *Journey's End*. By the end of the 1920s, before the opening of the Odeon or the Savoy, there were already four cinemas in the city centre – the City Palace (Fore Street), the Empire Electric (High Street), the Hippodrome (London Inn Square) and the Palladium (Paris Street) – as well as the King's Hall across the river in Okehampton

Street. In one week in 1928 the Empire offered *The King of Kings*, the Palladium *The White Slave* and *The Patent Leather Kid*, the City Palace *The Better Way* and *Passion's Fool*, and the King's Hall *A Country Doctor* and *Almost Human*. The centre of the town was so busy in the late evening that Councillor Alford proposed that the trams should continue later in the evening, claiming that there could be '500 or 600 people coming from the Hippodrome Theatre and other places of entertainment after 10.00 at night, with no trams to take them home'.

52 *Trams brought people into the city centre for events such as horticultural shows held at the Civic Hall in Queen Street.*

Local People Remember Exeter Trams and the People Who Worked on Them

In response to a local appeal at history events and in local newspapers in the autumn of 2008, several people have shared their memories of the trams, and of their family connections with the trams. People who remember the trams themselves included …

Former mayor Bill Hallett (W. J. Hallett), who spoke to the Civic Society in 2002 about his memories of the trams. His family lived in Heavitree Park and he attended the Maynard Junior School. He remembered the trams as very scruffy. The conductor would stamp on the bell to signal 'Go'. The schoolboys stood on the bell, driving the conductor mad. Bill would put little stones in the tram track to see if they got ground to dust. Once he put one in just before he got on, and the tram wouldn't move.

John Vowler, who was allowed to 'drive' a tram as a schoolboy.

R.J. Michelmore, who wrote: 'I was brought up in Exeter … We lived at 93 Heavitree Road, a few houses down from Livery Dole, where there was a stop. The trams reversed at the top of the hill beyond Heavitree Park, where the conductor had to swing the pole to reverse on the wire. The greatest thrill was getting up to the front of the open-top deck, when it was going down Fore Street. You appeared to be in front of the driver. There was a screeching noise from the wheels in the rails, especially on corners, which was accompanied by the constant ringing of the bell.'

Denis A. Ware, who wrote: 'I was born in May 1918 in the large flat over what was then the Exeter Public Dispensary, where my father was secretary and head dispenser until 1925/6. The trams ran all day along Queen Street, and as a small boy I could watch them, and the other, largely horse-drawn vehicles, from the "sitting-room" windows. The trams were open-topped and ran down to St David's station, to and fro all day until past my bedtime. I was given a conductor's toy outfit at some time and collected tram tickets when I was sometimes taken on a trip to watch the trains. Passengers put their old tickets through a slot by the platform, and they dropped into a little cupboard which had a door next to the first seat inside. I could open the door if I sat there and remove a selection to put on my clip.

'We occasionally went on the tram to "The Fountain" at the top of Sidwell Street, as my maternal grandparents lived at St James. There was a small wooden hut there where the crew could have a break. I believe this was the end of the double track, but some trams went up to Mount Pleasant Road, but not down Pinhoe Road as far as I can remember. We rarely went "up top", but when we did I liked to watch the driver swing the trolley arm around when it was a return journey. I would try to step on the driver's foot-knob, which rang the warning gong, under the front bumper and had to stand on the seat to reach the bell cord if we wanted to get off at the next stop.'

People whose families were involved with working on the trams included …

Margaret Batten, who wrote about her father Gilbert Easterbrooke (*above*). Gil was a tram conductor, a tram driver and then one of the first bus drivers in Exeter. She told us that the drivers and their conductors worked as pairs for years.

Frank Potter, who wrote: 'My grandfather, Frank Henry Potter, who died in 1942, worked on the trams in some capacity, and I enclose a photograph of him taken, I would guess, about the time of the First World War when he would have been forty or so. His uniform has the number ECT 19. Earlier censuses and certificates show that he was a coachman/gardener employed by a family in New North Road.'

Pat Vaughan, whose father Jack Tucker started as a blacksmith's apprentice and then became a conductor on the trams and later a driver on the buses. Jack Tucker was very active in the social club and helped to get a club house built next to the Paris Street depot after the First World War. Plates 54 and 55 on p. 72 show Jack Tucker at two different stages in his career.

Pat Parker, whose mother Helen Harris was one of the first 'motormaids': 'Helen Harris and the other conductresses had to work in all weathers, including clambering up and down from the tram to change the points manually. She tried wearing puttees to keep warm and dry, but they were always becoming tangled up, so she made breeches to wear beneath her long navy uniform skirt. She would sometimes "overlook" a couple of sweethearts seeking privacy on the top deck and "forget" to collect their fares.'

WORKING ON THE TRAMS

*Staff numbers in the service
grew from 56 in 1905
to 180 in 1930. Most staff
seemed to have enjoyed their
work and the social life
of the staff club.*

Over the twenty-six years of its operation the city council's tramways undertaking substantially increased its numbers of employees. After recruiting a manager, the initial complement of staff at Exeter Corporation Tramways consisted of sixteen motormen and sixteen conductors (working a fifty-four-hour week), an outdoor inspector and two track cleaners. In the depot there was a foreman (working sixty hours, including night work), a fitter, a

53 *Tramways staff (and friends) pose with a new car before it goes into service.*

labourer and a 'boy'. In the office there was a head clerk, a ticket clerk and a shorthand clerk. Arthur Nicholls was appointed as the first chief driver and instructor, and was to serve as motorman no. 1 until the trams were withdrawn twenty-five years later. Several of the staff were recruited from the old Exeter Tramways Company. When the tramways enterprise ended in 1931, Councillor Bradley (the Tramways Committee chairman) said that in 1905 there had

been a staff of fifty-six and their weekly wages were £54. Now there
were 180 and their weekly wages were £450.

Initial work to develop the tramways was undertaken by the
city engineers, Thomas Moulding and H.D. Munro, followed by
the appointment of W. Hedderstedt in overall charge. The first
tramway manager was H.C. Bartlett. He was replaced in 1917 by
R.O. Baldwin, and then by W.Y. Smith-Saville who saw through the
tram service into the era of the buses.

The Tramways Committee were regularly engaged in sorting
out terms and conditions. Early in 1905, just before electrification,
the bishop and a deputation petitioned the corporation not to run
the trams on Sundays, which they claimed should be a 'day of rest'
for the staff. The potential loss of revenue was too severe for the
corporation to agree, but trams on Sundays did not start until the
early afternoon. The opening of the Alphington Road extension led
to an enquiry about the need for a shelter for staff at the terminus.
The town clerk reported that the men preferred tea or coffee to be
brought to them in cans from their homes so that they could drink
it when they chose.

Disputes were also reported. The Transport and General
Workers' Union were often involved between the wars in resolving
issues such as staff suspensions or the reinstatement of those who
had joined the General Strike in 1926. But staff seem generally to
have enjoyed their roles and to have stayed with the trams for years,
as the photographs of Jack Tucker (see plates 54 and 55, p.72) show.

The numbers of staff were enough for them to run their own
social and sporting activities, first on an informal basis, described as

54 (above) *Young Jack Tucker in his first tramways uniform.*

55 (above right) *Jack Tucker, in 'summer uniform' with a white-topped cap, poses with one of the fitters and a schoolboy driver 'having a go' at tram-driving inside the depot.*

'starting with a game of draughts', and then acquiring a bagatelle board and later a full-sized billiard table. Later, in 1917, perhaps as a means of improving staff morale, a meeting was held to promote the formation of the Exeter Corporation Tramways Athletic and Social Society. Mr Blower, the depot superintendent presided, and Mr F. Vaughan became the first secretary.

One of the first big events following the inauguration was held on New Year's Eve, 1917 with a prize whist drive and a social. Refreshments were served, with one of the waiters 'impersonating Charlie Chaplin and taking a great fancy to the

56 *Outings for staff and their families were a popular activity of the Exeter Corporation Tramways staff club.*

conductresses'. The *Express and Echo* recorded that the entertainment included pianoforte selections, flute and songs (including some from Mrs H.M. Harris). The playing of *Auld Lang Syne* was followed by Mr Bushell, who 'gave a very smart turn with the punch ball, delighting the company with his smartness', and the party wound up with a dance. In 1923, by which time the society was called the 'Recreation Club', the mayor opened a new Recreation Room at the depot.

One young man, Albert Wotton, appears to have been identified so closely with his job that his family chose to have a tram carved on his memorial stone in the Higher Cemetery after his tragically early death from food poisoning. Frank Potter, who drew attention to this gravestone (see plate 57, *right*), noted that at the inquest Albert Wotton was found to have been under-nourished and wondered whether the hard routine of tram work had contributed to his state.

57 *Headstone of Albert Wotton in Exeter's Higher Cemetery. Wotton died at the age of nineteen in 1913, and his parents chose to commemorate him with the carving of a tram on his stone.*

58 *Detail of the motorman's uniform, taken from an early photograph of a tram in Queen Street, taken from Plate 52 on p.65.*

The details of the uniform did change from time to time, as the Tramways Committee determined, but male crew members seem always to have worn a peaked cap, self-coloured in the winter, white-topped in the summer and to have had 'ECT' for Exeter Corporation Tramways on both collars. Each motorman originally had two rows of brass buttons down the front of his jacket (see plate 58, *left*), while each conductor had his pouch for collecting fares, worn across one shoulder underneath an epaulette, and his ticket machine and clip for issuing tickets across the other (see plate 55, p.72).

The First World War and the Trams

The period of the First World War, from August 1914 to November 1918, was one of great difficulty for the trams. Almost 80 per cent of the staff undertook war service in one capacity or another, with 60 per cent serving overseas in the various theatres of war.

Men of military age in the corporation's service volunteered, or were later called up, leaving the trams short of staff. For the first time women were employed, as 'conductresses' or 'motormaids' and paid £1 a week, more than the boy conductors received. Being a 'motorman', however, was still perceived as a man's job, and the corporation were dependent on those not eligible for the army or over military age to fill the gaps. By mid-1917 trainees were paid £1 7s. a week as learners, with a war bonus of 2s. 6d. and after 'about two weeks' training were considered capable of taking out a car'. An experienced motorman could earn up to £1 15s. a week plus the 'war bonus'.

To cope with the problems of under-manning 'short running' was regularly practised, with trams terminating at stages such as the Exe Bridge, leaving passengers to walk on to their destination or to wait frustratedly at the terminus for trams that never came. Although the trams remained popular, with 91,000 journeys recorded in the week ending 18 January 1917, there were increasing grumbles about the way in which services were run when there were not enough crews to operate the full service. A passenger expecting to travel from the Guildhall to Alphington Road wrote to complain that the service he wanted to catch had without any warning terminated at Haven Road so that the car could return to service in the town. In January 1918 the daytime services were cut from a car every eight minutes to a car every nine minutes. Problems of unreliability continued, however, and

59 On 7 August 1914, just four days after the outbreak of the First World War, the Devon Regiment Reserves marched down Exeter High Street, holding up the trams as they went.

in October 1918 'Oft Disappointed' wrote to the *Express and Echo* complaining about late running and overcrowding on the trams. 'A motorman' responded that between the war and the flu it was only with difficulty that a service was provided at all. The general manager himself had been known to take a bag and a punch in order to relieve the conductors on duty.

Inability to afford or to obtain the materials for repairs meant that the track deteriorated. Journeys therefore were noisier and more uncomfortable, and this led to a rise in the electricity used and to the cost of the enterprise. In 1911 the cost of electrical power per car mile had been 1.233*d.* per car mile; by 1917 it was more than 1.5*d.* After the war, with better maintenance and more experienced drivers it reduced to 1.4*d.*

Most serious were the safety issues resulting from poor maintenance. It is probably no coincidence that Exeter's only tram accident involving a fatality occurred during this period, in March 1917.

The 1917 Accident

On 7 March 1917, tramcar no. 12, travelling from Heavitree to Dunsford Hill on the 11 a.m. service, went out of control down the steep incline of Fore Street. The driver, Charley Saunders, had the brakes full on, but they became disconnected and the tram continued to accelerate, colliding with a London and South Western Railway horse-drawn delivery wagon carrying tobacco and matches, which was pulling out to avoid a kerbside barrow. The

60 The worst tram accident in Exeter's history. Car no. 12 overturned on Exe Bridge, killing one passenger, Mary Findlay.

driver of the wagon, John Robinson, escaped death but the horse was thrown across the pavement into the shop fronts and killed. The tram conductress, Mrs Harle, jumped off in Bridge Street and escaped injury.

Charley Saunders, who was an experienced driver and a former coachman, kept his violently swaying vehicle upright, safely passing another tram on the journey up Fore Street. When the car reached Exe Bridge, however, it left the rails and, swerving to the right, hit the bridge parapet and turned over. The scene was photographed by various opportunists, including the photographer Henry Wykes who had his studios on New Bridge Street and immediately made up cards for sale from the photographs he had taken.

The accident took place at a quiet time of day, when the forty-two-seat tram had only five passengers on board – four women and a young man employed by the Tramways Committee who was the only passenger on the upper deck and prudently descended

the staircase as soon as the collision occurred. Four of the passengers escaped without serious injury, although three needed treatment at the Royal Devon and Exeter Hospital. Unfortunately one woman, Mary Findlay, was killed. Mary Findlay is buried in the Higher Cemetery.

The Board of Trade were satisfied that this was a freak accident rather than the result of service deficiencies and no public inquiry was held. The inquest confirmed the verdict of accidental death.

61 Mary Findlay, like Albert Wotton, was buried in Exeter's Higher Cemetery. By coincidence her stone also is carved with the quotation 'Peace, Perfect Peace'.

The accident in March 1917 was not the only one involving Exeter's trams. Only a few months later, in August, there was the report of a tramcar jumping the points in Fore Street, Heavitree just below the Royal Oak. It hit a house on the southern side of the street, demolishing its garden rails and porch. The driver, Samuel Warr, 'kept perfectly cool' and applied the brakes instantly and the passengers were frightened but uninjured. The *Express and Echo* reported that this had happened earlier at the same place, which caused comment in the locality about the dangerous condition of the rails, although it was thought that on this occasion the accident was due to a stone becoming lodged in the rail. The company later issued a denial that the magnetic or hand brakes were faulty or that the driver was travelling too fast or that the tram jumped the points because they were silted up with mud.

This incident prompted an editorial in the *Express and Echo* on 14 August, which mentioned 'the number of accidents, large and small, that constantly occur'. The same page of the council's press-cuttings book that contains this editorial recorded two further accidents. One was down to 'a youth' who had placed detonators, apparently fog signals stolen from the London and South Western Railway, on the tram rails in Blackboy Road and Heavitree Road, causing 'much alarm' to passengers when the tram went over them. He claimed that this was done merely 'in fun' and denied a similar offence of placing seven detonators on the track in the Pinhoe Road, but Exeter Police Court fined him 10s. for the offence.

Some accidents could not be attributable to poor maintenance. Mabel Huggins had her bicycle wheels caught in the tram line points when trying to pass a wagon near the Post Office in the High Street and was thrown from her bike. Alice Penfold, described as a gipsy, was driving her wagon over Exe Bridge when her horse took fright at a tramcar. It bolted, she fell off and two wheels of the wagon ran her over. Layman, a young conductor who had dismounted at the High Street tram stop

62 *A tram has run off the rails in Heavitree and ended up almost coming through the front door of the terraced house.*

outside Walton's and was chatting to the driver, was crushed between the tram and a horse-drawn wagon pulling out of the Cathedral Yard. He was taken off in the police ambulance for treatment at the Royal Devon and Exeter Hospital.

The *Express and Echo* laid most of the blame for accidents on the inexperience of the crews and also on what it called their spirit of 'don't care'. The editorial commented that the staff, with the exception of the tram shed staff, had 'no apparent interest in the concern' and noted a number of problems with lack of courtesy, lack of collection of fares and insubordination 'People get on the trams and they leave the trams and they do not pay because there is nobody in evidence to whom they can pay their fare' ... 'I have seen ... a motorman driving up the street with one hand on his control and the other holding an apple, the while he is engaged in a vigorous conversation with the conductress.'

In 1917 the Tramways Committee recognised what the *Express and Echo* called 'the very unsatisfactory state of affairs in regard to the personnel as well as the equipment of our Exeter Tramways' and decided to replace the manager, Mr H.C. Bartlett, who had been in post since 1905, with a new manager, Mr R.O. Baldwin, who moved to Exeter from Bournemouth. This did not immediately lead to industrial peace. Requests by the employees for a pay rise were met by a council decision to increase wages for the drivers by 2s. 6d. a week and a smaller rise for 'the boys', but no rise for the conductresses, the 'shed staff' or the inspectors. This led to a further meeting of the staff and a call for strike action if wages were not increased by 20 per cent for all grades. The award went to national arbitration and the settlement included an award to women aged eighteen and over and more generous terms overall. The threat of a strike was averted. Mr Baldwin proved an excellent acquisition. He was apparently the 'worst-paid corporation tramways manager in Britain', though, and it was not until 1920 that his pay was raised to £400.

Getting Back to Normal: The Trams after the War

The return of drivers from military service enabled the tram frequencies to increase again to every seven and a half minutes, although in 1919 the Tramways Committee still had to be cautious about the amount of electrical current they used. The St David's service ran at a six-minute frequency, but the committee could not immediately reintroduce the Sunday service. The committee was also spending again on purchasing rails, points and crossings for repairs – by April 1919 they had spent £4,000.

By 1919 demobilisation allowed some at least of the vacant posts to be filled by experienced staff. Some had become too old to be conductors or drivers, and one man at least had become so deaf that he was considered to be a potential risk as a driver, but other work was found for these men in the depot. Weekday services improved, with frequencies up to every seven and a half minutes. However, the trams were using almost all the electric current permitted on the weekday service alone, and the reintroduction of Sunday services continued to be delayed. In 1921, with continuing problems over current, the committee agreed that for a period the evening services should be operated by the Devon General Omnibus and Touring Company, which would run motor bus services very much along the tram routes.

Fares needed to rise to keep pace with the increased costs. This was not just a question of paying increased wages. The committee heard about fittings that had risen in price by up to 500 per cent. The Ministry of Transport approved a rise in fares and the fare structure was changed – much to the disappointment of some councillors – so that fares from the Guildhall were 1*d*. to Exe Bridge, to the depot in Heavitree Road and to Belmont, and then 1½*d*. to the end of the line. Passenger numbers rose and in 1919/1920, with almost six million journeys taken, exceeded those of the days before the war. Fares were kept under review and arrangements for cheap 'workmen's fares' and 'return fares' confirmed by the committee.

Repairs in the depot had meanwhile speeded up, and the manager, Mr Baldwin, aspired to run a five-minute service, which he trialled in August 1920, prior to the arrival of the two additional cars that the committee had authorised. Plans were set in hand to extend the workshop areas at the depot, and the new extension was opened in June 1923, including the latest machinery: 'an apparatus for shrinking tyres on wheel centres, a wheel press for pressing off axles, a lathe for turning armatures, car axles and bearings, a power hacksaw for sawing steel bars and bench shears for cutting sheet metal'.

But it was not just the tramcars that required investment to deal with the backlog in maintenance. The council were pleased to note

63 One of the fitters from the depot undertaking 'running repairs' as the tram passes the depot.

a surplus made on the operation of the trams in 1921 but agreed that part of this should be devoted to repairs to Cowick Street, which was 'in a very bad state … one of the worst in the city, and the traffic was enormous'. The tramways undertaking bore about one-third of the cost of road repairs along the tram routes, but found that poor repairs outside the tracks, such as were identified in 1921 along the Heavitree route, meant that the road was full of potholes, and cyclists and others kept to the tram tracks in order to avoid them, thus increasing the wear and tear on the tramway. Money was finally earmarked for Cowick Street repairs at the end of 1922.

In order to achieve the more frequent running that Mr Baldwin and the committee desired, it was

64 To deal with the growing fleet of trams and the complexity of their maintenance, the original depot was extended in 1923 with the addition of new workshops.

agreed that some of the track should be doubled to allow passing. The High Street was an early target for improvement. Agreement was reached in 1923 that the track should be doubled from the Post Office to Bedford Street, although some councillors considered that this was unlikely to solve the growing problem of traffic congestion, and they pressed, without success, for the doubled track to be extended further along the High Street to the Guildhall.

Alderman Ross, true to form, suggested, amid council laughter, that instead of spending money on improving the track, the High Street should be 'closed to all vehicles except the trams'.

The Chair of the Tramways Committee, Councillor F. Chick, deftly sidestepped this proposal, reminding Alderman Ross, whose shop was in the High Street, that 'since the trams had been in the High Street the value of the property in that thoroughfare had increased enormously'.

TRAMS AND THE STREET SCENE

Exeter's trams ran from Mount Pleasant to Alphington Road, from Cross Park in Heavitree to the end of Cowick Street, and from the High Street down to St David's station.

Tram Routes of Exeter Tramways Company, 1882–1905

When Exeter Tramways Company first set up its horse-drawn operations, the opposition to the running of trams along the High Street meant that the centre of tram operations developed beyond the original site of the East Gate. The meeting point where the tram routes intersected was London Inn Square, which was at the former staggered junction of the High Street, Paris Street, Sidwell Street and New North Road (see plate 65, *below*).

65 London Inn Square was an important hub for Exeter's roads and traffic from coaching days until this area of the city was replanned after the Exeter blitz.

The first horse-drawn tram in 1882 ran from the Bude Hotel on London Inn Square to Midway Terrace on Heavitree Road, close to the then St Luke's College, now the St Luke's campus of the University of Exeter. (J.C. Gillham's plan of the horse-tram routes is shown in plate 10, p.18.) This route was extended in May 1883 on to Livery Dole at the edge of Heavitree itself. Also in 1883 additional routes from London Inn Square were introduced. The first ran along New North Road past 'the obelisk', replaced in 1897 by the Miles Memorial Clock Tower, down Hele Road to St David's station. The second tram route was along Sidwell Street (where opposition from

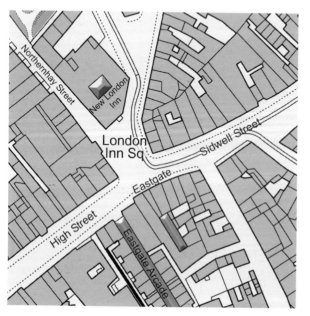

the traders was more muted) and up to the top of the Bath Road, later to become Blackboy Road.

Under a short-lived experiment in 1897, a horse-drawn bus service ran along Old Tiverton Road and Union Road, but this was not a success. Nor was business successful enough to prompt the owners to take up the approval that they had been given to run an extension down Queen Street to the junction with the High Street. In fact the services to and from the station were so poorly used that the company were driven to reduce it so that it finally ran only on market days.

Tram Routes of Exeter Corporation Tramways, 1905–1931

66 This view of the Clock Tower was taken in June 1904 and clearly shows the tram lines down New North Road, a route used only by the horse-drawn trams.

An ambitious scheme that led to the introduction of the electric trams was submitted for approval as part of the Exeter Corporation Tramways Act in 1903. The long-running opposition to the service in the High Street was finally ended by popular vote, and it was then agreed that the new electric trams should run along the High Street and down Fore Street and over the new Exe Bridge. After Exe Bridge the tracks divided. One route ran as far as Stone Lane on Alphington Road. The other began the climb up the hill as far as the Falmouth Inn (in 2009 the 'First and Last') at the top of Cowick Street, where the former turnpike had begun. The Heavitree terminus for the Cowick Street service was at Cross

Park Terrace, in Fore Street (Heavitree) between the entrance to the Heavitree Pleasure Ground and Victor Place. The Pinhoe Road service from the Alphington Road terminated just beyond the Mount Pleasant Inn corner, at Abbey Road. Services from St David's station sometimes terminated in Queen Street but at other times ran on as far as Pinhoe Road.

As well as those sections of the planned routes that were actually constructed, the official approval had included a number of possible extensions. These would have created a tramway from the High Street down Eastgate as far as Southernhay; one route down Longbrook Street and up to Pennsylvania Road and Union Road; another one along Bonhay from St David's to Fore Street; and two other tramways – one along Denmark Road from Magdalen

67 (below) The Alphington branch ended out at Stone Lane on the Alphington Road. The greenhouses of the nurseries there can be seen in this scene.

68 (above) The Cowick Street branch ended where the steep climb of Dunsford Hill began, at the junction with Buddle Lane.

69 (left) *The Pinhoe Road line ran out beyond the location of the earlier turnpike gate over the crest of the hill as far as Abbey Road.*

70 (above) *The Heavitree line ran through Fore Street, Heavitree and on as far as Cross Park.*

Street and the other down South Street to Weirfield Road. The corporation was careful to ensure the profitability of its service, however, and these were never constructed.

On the Pinhoe side of the city a further extension to the old horse-drawn track was made. The new tram route ran down from the Mount Pleasant Inn as far as Abbey Road. Both St David's and Queen Street (Central) stations were now linked to the city centre by a track that ran along Queen Street to the High Street, a major construction feat that stopped traffic in the city for weeks (see plate 15, p.29). The old horse-tram route along New North Road was abandoned.

Although the area across the river served by the trams had been part of the city since the incorporation of the St Thomas district within the city boundaries in 1899, at the time when the electric trams were first introduced the city boundary with Heavitree was still set at Livery Dole. A formal agreement had to be made in 1905 for the corporation to be able to exercise running powers over the Heavitree streets so that the new trams could run through Heavitree as far as Cross Park.

Where to Catch the Tram

Once the tram routes and their terminuses were agreed, the question of where along the route the trams should stop became an issue. Each stop was given a name. The list agreed in 1905 for the Heavitree route out from the centre, for example, set them out as Bedford Street, Sidwell Junction, Depot, Gladstone Road, Grendon Road, Barrack Road, Gordon Lamp, Church Street, Butts Lane for South Wonford, and Terminus (for East Wonford).

Local people lobbied via petitions to get stops placed nearby or in the most convenient locations in the centre of the city. There were petitions: for all trams into or out of the centre to stop at the Carfax; for Pinhoe–Alphington trams to stop at St Sidwell's Church in Sidwell Street and at Ladysmith Road (Commins Road); and for trams to stop in Paris Street, on Heavitree Hill and at Church Street on the Heavitree route. The result was that there were a large number of stopping places. Between the end of Sidwell Street and Alphington Street, for example, there were thirteen regular tram stops and six request stops.

As the city continued to spread into its ring of residential suburbs there were proposals for expanding the network of tram routes. South Street and Holloway Street residents and those

living along Bonhay Road between Exe Bridge and St David's
station asked for new routes. The possibility of extending the
services down Longbrook Street up to Union Road was discussed,
but no such new routes were developed. Even the additions and
extensions that had been drafted while legislation for the service
was under way were never built. Later, after the First World War,
more serious consideration was given to an extension in Heavitree
to Hamlyn Lane, and from Pinhoe Road out to Whipton, but
neither was finally agreed, although the Pinhoe Road extension got
as far as Ministry of Transport approval for a loan. Thus the limits
of the electric tram network in 1931 were the same as the original
ones laid down in 1905.

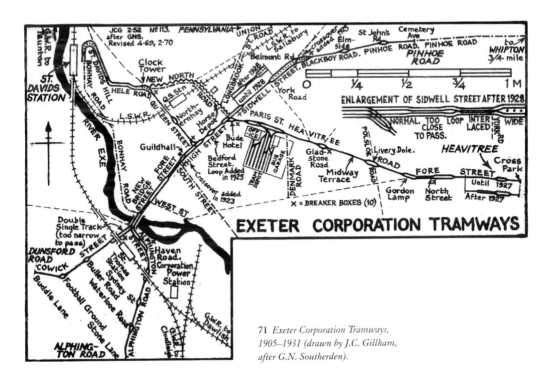

71 *Exeter Corporation Tramways,*
1905–1931 (drawn by J.C. Gillham,
after G.N. Southerden).

Touring the City

Worth's City Guide, published in the 1920s, gives suggestions of
tram rides that visitors could take to see points of particular interest.
The corporation themselves were keen to promote tourism and
made sure that the first timetable published included a list of
notable sights – the Guildhall, the Cathedral, Northernhay.

Worth's City Guide recommended:

RIDE NO. 1

Starting from Guildhall, take Car marked Heavitree (Red Disc), 1½ miles, which
passes through main street. Notice quaint old Houses and Churches. Thence along a
pleasant open road by St Luke's Training College (for Schoolmasters), past Livery Dole
(the site on which years ago John Bennett M.A., was burnt for heresy), by the Gordon
Memorial Lamp, down a steep decline into Heavitree (one of the last places visited by
the late General Gordon). If time permits, wander into the new Pleasure Grounds.

RIDE NO. 2

Starting from Guildhall, take Car marked Dunsford Road (Red Disc). Notice quaint
Houses en route – Hinton Lake's, Stocker's, Old Guildhall, Old Statue of St Peter
(corner of North Street, on right), Cavaliers' House (on left), then St Olave's Church (on
right), St John's (on left), Tuckers' Hall (right), down a steep decline over the new steel
Exe Bridge (designed by Sir John Wolfe Barry, K.C.B.), over the River into St Thomas,
past the quaint old Parish Church to Dunsford Gate, and then for a glorious walk into
the Country to Ide, back around Alphington.

RIDE NO. 3

Starting at Guildhall, take Pinhoe Road Car (Green Disc). Pass through main street,
notice *Express and Echo* Office, Ross' House, St Stephen's Church, St Lawrence's Church,
Karslake's quaint Frontage, the Arcade, and St Sidwell's Church.

Track and Track Improvements

The initial trackway laid for the horse-drawn trams was 3ft 6in in gauge. High standards were set by the Board of Trade, and the initial visit by their inspector in April 1882 resulted in the issue of an order for remedial work to be undertaken. This delayed the opening of the section between St Luke's College and Livery Dole.

The trackway for the electric trams maintained the 3ft 6in gauge, but the track itself was of a heavier weight. Messrs Ireland of Morecambe were responsible for the construction, which was made of girder-type steel rails, 6in deep and weighing 90lb per linear yard. Some of the original tram rails manufactured for the opening of the electric tram service still exist, recycled for use to prop up the wall of one of the old warehouses down at the Quay (see plate 73, p.94).

72 Section of tram rail dug up during recent road repairs at Hele Road and preserved by Dick Passmore.

The foundation for the rails and paving was of cement concrete, 6in thick. In addition to this concrete underbed, the rails were packed up to the true alignment by fine cement concrete, averaging 3/4in thick. The points and crossings were made of patent manganese steel. The gradient for the track was generally flat, but on St David's Hill it was 1 in 16 and on Fore Street as much as 1 in 11.5.

The track was set either between a paving of granite setts, with an 18in margin of setts at each outer edge, or across wooden blocks,

73 Tram rails recycled and used as buttressing for a building on Exeter Quay. Close inspection of the rails reveals the date 1904, showing that this was part of the track laid for the electric tram service.

which were thought to be less noisy. Hazel Harvey in *Discovering Exeter: Sidwell Street* quoted from Mr H. Aggett, who remembered 'the trams clattering up through – bang, bang, bang; the tram chaps'd stamp their feet on the bell'. The noise was obviously considerably to the annoyance of some residents. There was a petition for the streets to be laid with wooden blocks instead of granite setts along Alphington Road. Alderman Lucas complained in 1930 that 'the noise was such that he could not work in his office. He had to leave it that morning. At Bath, where there was wood block paving, there was no noise.' The noise increased as the rails wore down and became corrugated.

The initial stretch of track constructed for the horse-drawn trams was 2³/8th miles. This was extended for the electric tramways – according to the commemorative brochure published to celebrate their opening – to 4¹/4 street miles in length and consisted of 2¹/8 miles of double line and 2¹/8 miles of single line with passing places. The total length of track at the time the services closed was almost 5 miles.

Double lines and interlacing lines were constructed on what were expected to be the busiest streets, where there would be the greatest amount of additional traffic, such as the western section of the High Street and Fore Street, in spite of their relatively narrow width from kerb to kerb. Otherwise passing loops were built. In

Sidwell Street, and also in Cowick Street, there was a strange track layout with the doubled tracks laid so close to each other that no two cars could safely pass. From St Sidwell's Church there was an 80ft loop followed by 230ft of the interlaced track opening out to normal double line at York Road. A similar arrangement existed in Cowick Street between the Exe Bridge and St Thomas railway station. The most likely reason for the 'loop' outside St Sidwell's Church in Sidwell Street (see plate 74, *below*) seems to have been to make savings on the installation of points.

At the Bude Hotel and Exe Bridge junctions, the points were operated electrically by the driver from the tram. At the High Street and depot junctions they were changed manually using a point iron. On other passing loops the points were permanently sprung to the left.

Over time, the economical approach to the laying of the initial tracks, which meant that single-line tracks had been laid wherever possible, proved to have been short-sighted. The delays that were caused by trams waiting to be allowed to enter single-track sections meant that track had to be doubled in the Blackboy Road in 1915. Between 1925 and 1927 the tracks were doubled in Sidwell Street with a loop-line crossover at St Ann's Chapel. Approvals had also been secured for the doubling of the

74 The start of the 'loop' in Sidwell Street. The tracks were too close together for trams actually to pass each other, but the expense of additional points was saved.

75 A car was used to provide temporary shelter from the weather for passengers forced to change trams in order to avoid the track repairs in Queen Street.

track in Cowick Street, though this was never undertaken.

Maintenance of the tracks made continuing demands on the Tramways Committee's expenditure. While repairs were under way at the Clock Tower junction, passengers were expected to change trams, and a car acted as a waiting room for passengers transferring from one section to another of the service (see plate 75, *left*).

It was always difficult for the corporation to keep pace with the expenditure required for maintenance. The serious situation the track had reached by 1928 was set out in the final report that provided the background for the decision to change over from trams to buses. The expert consultant engaged by the corporation listed the short-term maintenance work needed, which included the relaying of track along Alphington Road, along Pinhoe Road down from Mount Pleasant to the terminus, down St David's Hill and in Paris Street. Together with the need to deal with grinding corrugations, the maintenance bill that the city was facing would have cost more than £12,000 (about £450,000 at present-day prices).

The Overhead Power Supply and Cabling

Current for the operation of the trams was generated by the city's own power station at Haven Banks, which had been constructed in 1901. It had superseded an earlier one and provided a total output of 1,300kW. The current was provided as AC output, which rotary converters modified to provide the tramways with current at 500–550 volts DC. The tramways were a welcome addition to the needs of the city for electricity as they took the majority of their supply during daylight hours, when the demand for electricity was otherwise at its lowest.

76 *The Haven Banks Power Station housed state-of-the-art generating equipment when it was first constructed in 1902.*

The trams were supplied with electricity by means of a trolley pole on the upper deck, which drew the power from overhead cables, using round-section 4–0 wire with soldered ears in an orthodox overhead trolley system with swivel heads. The traction poles were mainly of the side-bracket type, although there were elegant central poles with wrought-iron scroll work in Sidwell Street between York Road and Belmont Road and down St David's

Hill to the station. Some poles doubled as part of the street lighting system and remained in use for a period after the trams had been withdrawn. Keen eyes can still spot some of the round bases for the poles left to serve a different purpose amongst the railings on the left-hand side of the descent from the Buller Statue down Hele Road (see plate 78, *below*).

77 (left) *The traction poles carrying wires for the trams were generally located on one side or the other of the roadway. Where there was space, as here in Sidwell Street, a more ornate central pole was used.*

78 (right) *A further example of recycling appears in this incorporation of the base of a traction pole into the railings beside the pavement in Hele Road.*

79 *The corporation took advantage of the rebuilding of Exe Bridge in 1905 to incorporate combined lighting and traction poles into the design of the bridge parapet.*

The 1905 Exe Bridge was designed in such a way as to incorporate the poles for the overhead wiring and street lighting in the bridge parapet (see plate 79, *above*). One of these ornate traction standards has been preserved and now forms a landmark down on Exeter Quay (see plate 80, *right*). The Alphington section, which was completed later than the original track layout, had different ornate ironwork on the roadside traction poles (see plate 81, p.100).

Tram supply was controlled by means of section pillars. Current fed here in conduit from the generating station was conducted up the tramway pole to the overhead trolley line. One of the last section pillars to survive was at the Gervase Avenue junction at the end of Exe Bridge (see plate 82, p.100). Each 'section' (about half a mile in length) was separately supplied and could be isolated from

80 *After the replacement of the 1905 Exe Bridge by a new bridge layout, opened in 1971, some of the lamp standards from the old bridge were moved to new locations on the Quay.*

81 (right) *The later date of the construction of the tramway along Alphington Street and Alphington Road brought minor changes to the design of the roadside traction poles.*

82 (far right) *Section pillars, such as the one pictured here from the end of Exe Bridge, were fed by cables from the central electricity generating station. The current was then conducted up the tramway pole to the overhead trolley line.*

83 (above) *The railway bridges over Cowick Street (seen here) and Alphington Street were so low that the trams needed to lower their poles when passing beneath them.*

the rest of the route. The pillars were linked by telephone to the generating station and the depot so that faults could be quickly reported.

The railway line ran across both Cowick Street and Alphington Road on low bridges. These were one of the reasons why the top deck of the trams was never covered in. The bridges were so low that the trams had to lower their poles when passing under them (see plate 83, *left*), and the bridges themselves carried a warning notice for passengers to keep in their seats, please!

Timetables, Fares and Tickets

Timetables were subject to constant consideration and revision. Broadly the electric tram service ran from 7.15 a.m. to 11.00 p.m. on weekdays and from 1.30 to 10.00 p.m. on Sundays. Trams had to run quietly on Sundays so as to avoid making unnecessary noise during the times of church and chapel services. From the start of the tram service the timetables were published in newspapers such as the *Flying Post*. The photographs (in plate 84, *below*) show a sample timetable for the early morning runs on the Heavitree–Dunsford Road line, dating from 1923. The timetable cover was red on this occasion, although this was not always the case for the Heavitree line and an earlier timetable, dating from October 1922 and the introduction of more frequent services, had a pink cover.

The horse-drawn trams charged a universal fare of 1*d*. for a journey, with a through fare of 3*d*. for those travelling across

84 *Timetables like this one from the 1920s had sturdy coloured covers (this one is red). Changes to timetables and the need to reprint meant that the later timetables were never of the quality of the early ones, in which the corporation advertised the sights to see in Exeter.*

E.C.T.

HEAVITREE
AND
DUNSFORD ROAD

8¼, 6¼, 7½ Minutes' Service.

Extended 6¼ Minutes' Service.

9-7-23,
14-7-23.

W.T. No. 212

London Inn Square to and from St David's station as well as on the Heavitree or Sidwell Street sections. The original fare structure on the electric trams from the outer termini to the Guildhall was 1¹/₂d. except for Heavitree, which was 2d. From one terminus to another terminus could be 1¹/₂d., 2d. or 2¹/₂d. A special cheap fare known as a 'workmen's' single or return could be used so long as the outer journey was completed by 9.00 a.m. and the return was between 5.00 and 6.00 p.m., or on Saturdays, when half-day working was usual, the return journey was made between 12.00 noon and 1.00 p.m. During the First World War servicemen were allowed to travel at half fare. From 1922 on, the fares were regularly reviewed.

Tickets for the electric tram system were first issued by the Tramways Purchase Syndicate and then by the corporation itself. Shades of salmon, blue, green or white were originally used for the tickets, and a large 'R' indicated a return ticket.

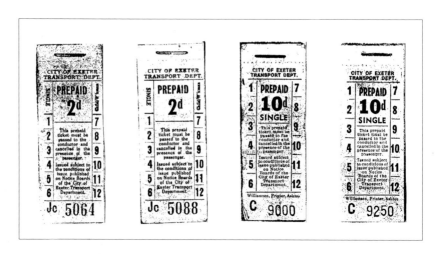

85 Tickets varied in colour according to cost and whether or not the journey was at a concessionary 'workmen's' fare. These tickets are green (2d.) or buff (10d.).

THE LAST DAYS OF THE TRAMS

*As motor vehicle numbers
increased, trams became part
of the problem of congestion
in the High Street and on Exe
Bridge. In 1931 they were
replaced by motor buses.*

The Growth of Petrol-driven Traffic

The trams continued to ply their trade reliably, generally speaking, even in the worst of weather (see, for example, plate 86, *below*). Many local people would have found it difficult to imagine life without them, particularly since the corporation ran their tram service as a monopoly and did not allow competition from private bus companies on the tram routes.

Trams were very much part of the everyday street scene. However, the street scene around them was changing. Even by the time the electric trams took over from the horse-drawn trams in 1905, vehicles driven by petrol engines, the new form of mechanical transport, were on the road, albeit in limited numbers. After the First World War the number of cars, vans and lorries began to increase dramatically. Twenty cars were registered in Exeter in the

86 *Car no. 10 climbing St David's Hill in the snow. The trams did their best to get through, whatever the weather.*

87 *Early days of the tram service in the High Street – the trams have the street almost completely to themselves.*

first full year of registration, 1904. By 1920 there were 140 new registrations, and the numbers continued to increase year on year. 'Cars', meaning motor-cars, were by then an everyday sight. A tram was jocularly referred to as a 'Workmen's Car'. The car and the 'Workmen's Car' had to cohabit in spaces that had never been designed to cope with anything wider, longer or faster than a cart or a carriage.

The High Street, a central stretch of the tram service, was the main thoroughfare of Exeter, just as it had been in medieval times. All the traffic heading for the river crossing at Exe Bridge, from the Bath and Honiton roads in one direction and the Plymouth, Torquay and Okehampton roads in the other, was funnelled through Fore Street and the High Street, meeting in the London Inn Square. The through traffic all had to make its way across Exe Bridge. This had been widened in

88 *Signs at the junction between Paris Street and Sidwell Street, the meeting point of the two roads from London: the Bath Road and the Honiton Road.*

1905 in readiness for the electric tram service, but was still only wide enough for one lane in either direction. As the chief constable told the Watch Committee in September 1929:

> On certain days at the height of the holiday season, and on Saturday mornings especially, traffic proceeding to or returning from south Devon or Cornwall arrives at one end or other of the central main street in a continuous stream which extends for miles back, and Alphington Street, Cowick Street, Sidwell Street and Paris Street have long lines of vehicles waiting to pass through the narrow main street.

The *Express and Echo* described the High Street as 'Pandemonium'. In 1929 Councillor Brock reported that he had been embarrassed while on holiday, because fellow motorists in his Cornish hotel had 'pestered' him for tips on the best way to get through Exeter on their journeys home.

The chief constable's traffic surveys, instituted in 1920 and undertaken every five years from that time, showed how things

DAILY TRAFFIC FLOWS IN EXETER HIGH STREET RECORDED BY POLICE CENSUS			
	1920	**1925**	**1930**
Horse-drawn vehicles and handcarts	1,386	1,296	522
Motor vehicles	1,314	3,403	5,901
Bicycles	2,340	3,252	3,000

were changing. By the end of the 1920s, the High Street was no longer able to cope adequately with the flow of the traffic that needed to use it, even out of the holiday season. It was generally accepted that something radical needed to be done to stop the city coming to a complete standstill. The city economy was dependent on its role as a centre to which people from the surrounding areas came to do their shopping or to use the professional services such as those provided by lawyers and accountants. If the city centre was not convenient to reach and easy to use, then trade would be lost. Yet, to some extent, this trade was itself the problem. There were delivery vans and lorries. There were private cars owned by people who expected, in the same way their parents and grandparents had been used to do in their carriages, to be able to stop directly outside the store they wanted to visit or the office of the professional man (or even woman) they wanted to consult.

As the *Express and Echo* put it in 1928:

Any morning of the week you may see scores – possibly up to a hundred – cars standing along the kerb in our main streets. There is a constant change of cars, as one goes off and another draws in, but cars are always there during the business hours … drawn up, not parked … the driver has left only for a panic-stricken minute or two whilst he or she rushes into a shop and dashes out again, half expecting to see a police officer standing by the car, note-book in hand.

On the general issue of traffic congestion, most councillors were agreed that something must be done. Not only were local businesses at risk of losing trade but also, as some like Councillor

Chilcott felt, even pedestrians were at risk of being knocked down in the narrow streets. He chafed against the corporation's natural inclination to do as little as possible. 'All they heard was … do as our grandfathers did. The people today are cussing because our grandfathers did not do what we have to do today.' On the other side of the argument were people like Alderman McGahey, who felt that solutions such as a bypass road would take 'the life blood' out of the city, tempting motorists with the chance to speed, 'like honey tempted a bee'. Exeter, said Councillor Thompson, depended on the people who came into it. If people were sent around Exeter the city would be on a byroad and soon on a branch railway.

The Search for Solutions

Broadly, there were four types of action the corporation could take. First, they could try to take some of the volume of the through traffic away from the High Street. They had built Prince of Wales Road to the north side of the city, to loop through between the Crediton and Tiverton roads (New North Road) and the Bath Road, via Union Road and Mount Pleasant. This, however, was not a success. The *Express and Echo* dismissed it as 'a charming promenade for citizens, but it isn't worth twopence as a relief to traffic congestion'. The corporation had also tried to develop the crossroads at Polsloe Bridge as a junction funnelling traffic away from Sidwell Street, with Hamlin Lane feeding off it one way and Monks Road another way. They devised a grand scheme to

cut through from the Pinhoe Road to Heavitree Road and down
Rifford Road to Topsham Road and thus across the marshes to
Alphington. In fact, though the corporation as a whole finally
decided in favour of this scheme, they were outmanoeuvred by the
county council, which had already secured ministry agreement to
the Hill Barton Road bypass down to Countess Wear, which ran
outside the city boundary. More radical schemes, never seriously
considered, contemplated a one-way system in the city centre,
with a second road parallel to the High Street, either developed
down Catherine Street and along the Cathedral Close, or down
Paul Street and Bartholomew Street through the West Quarter
to Exe Bridge. Anything of this kind would still have ended in a
bottleneck at Exe Bridge.

A second course of action was for the Watch Committee and
the police to introduce the traffic control measures that are so
familiar today. New road signs were erected to inform travellers
of the best (or least worst) route. The police, long responsible for
keeping order in the streets, began to find that keeping the traffic

89 *Police in Exeter in the 1930s practising the stop signal as part of their traffic signal drill in accordance with the newly developed Highway Code.*

flowing required new procedures. A new sign language had to be introduced: motorists had to learn it and police had to practise it (see plate 89, p.109). Traffic management came to occupy a substantial amount of constabulary time. The chief constable calculated in 1929 that he had at least ten officers employed on traffic duties every day, directing the traffic and dealing with obstructions. 'Automatic traffic signals' or 'traffic lights' as they are known today, began to be put in place, to supplement police constables. Signals were installed down at the Exe Bridge. Pressure came too to increase the number of designated parking places, with some people even proposing that leafy Bedford Circus should be bought up and taken over for this purpose.

As a third way forward the corporation began to consider the possibilities of instigating a one-way system for traffic involving Paris Street, Sidwell Street and Summerland Street. The Watch Committee were keen to try this before any more radical action was taken, but local business owners objected and forced a ministry inquiry, which led to the ministry ruling against the scheme. Some of those potentially affected told the ministry inspector that they felt the blame for congestion should be laid upon the trams: 'Remove the trams and you will get rid of all the trouble … They are a nuisance. Run buses.' There had been no congestion, they felt, when, two years earlier, in the General Strike of 1926 the tram service had been suspended. Once the ministry had ruled against the one-way system, the corporation continued to explore options for improvement in London Inn Square and ultimately, in 1933, two years after the trams had disappeared from the streets, ended

90 *By the end of the 1920s the pressures of the increasing numbers of motor cars, vans and lorries had led to frequent traffic jams along Exeter's High Street and over the Exe Bridge.*

up buying the Bude Hotel on the corner of Sidwell Street and Paris Street (see plate 90, *above*) in order to allow for street widening in the approach to the junction.

The corporation's final course of action was to enlist the help of the High Street traders in dealing with the growing volume of traffic. The mayor called a meeting with High Street traders in the autumn of 1928 and was ready with a list, provided by the chief constable, of things the traders could do to help. This included: rescheduling the times at which the shop received and despatched deliveries so that this

91 *Traffic problems at the Paris Street junction (see plate 88, p.105) led the corporation to buy and demolish the Bude Hotel in 1933.*

was done outside the peak periods for traffic; using the rear and side entrances rather than the main doors on to the High Street where this was feasible; and making sure that pavements were not obstructed by piles of crates and packages.

Councillor Cottey, who was also present, pointed out that parking along the roadside increased in the lunch hour, when the chauffeur-driven cars of the business owners waited to take the boss out for lunch. The mayor's private meeting, which had been mentioned in the paper, was gate-crashed by a number of citizens keen to make their views known about traffic generally, and the meeting quickly became a forum where everyone aired their pet solution to the traffic problems. The mayor and participants ended the discussion by referring the issue to the Chambers of Commerce and Trade for action, but not before someone mentioned the trams: 'Why couldn't the stops in the High Street be reorganised, with all down trams stopping at Bedford Circus and trams pulling right into the kerb at the Guildhall?'

Although the councillors were proud of their tram service, which had come back into profit during the 1920s, finally even they were convinced that the trams posed a real traffic problem. Part of its year-on-year profitability, after all, was due to a lack of investment in track renewal, although the manager had been able to persuade them to renew the tramcars.

Nonetheless the track was ageing, and this increased the noise the trams made running across the rails and blocks. 'Terrible', was how Councillor Hill described the noise in Paris Street, and when Alderman Lucas said he had had to leave his office in the High

Street because of the noise of repairs to the tram track in the High
Street, Alderman Stocker retorted that Mr Lucas should try coming
down to St Thomas and hear the noise there. Major investment
would soon be needed in the tram tracks themselves if the trams
were to continue. Nor could the corporation ignore the fact that
other councils around the country, faced with the same decision,
were changing over to petrol or trolley buses. Was Exeter going to
be left behind?

The Councillors Make Up Their Minds

The decision to give up the trams in favour of buses was not
easy for the corporation. By 1928 the Tramways Committee was
developing a complementary bus service to serve the areas the
trams did not reach, particularly the new estates in St Thomas,
Wonford and Whipton. Potential passengers, as well as the
councillors who would take the decision, got the chance to try
out a range of buses lent by other local authorities or supplied by
the manufacturers. The general verdict was that there was little
to choose between them, though some had more knee room than
others, and all seemed steep to climb into after the broad low
platforms of the trams. With the possible difficulties of Exeter's
hills in mind the buses were tried out on a test run up Pennsylvania
Road and down Rosebarn Lane. The councillors eventually
selected the AEC Regent III, which was well regarded in service in
other authorities.

The committee discussed the results of the trial and presented to the council in December 1928 a scheme for the next few years. 'Wait and see' was their recommendation on the future of the tramways, but in the meantime they recommended that the council should build the Pinhoe extension, expanding the service beyond the terminus at Abbey Road all the way to the new city boundary in Whipton. This indecisive approach did not find favour with the council. After a long discussion in which the defenders of the trams stoutly protested that citizens would not stand for the scrapping of the trams, and that buses would be unable to cope, it was agreed that the time had come for an expert report on the future of the system. In the meantime, no significant new expenditure should be incurred.

The independent expert selected was Mr A.R. Fearnley, the

EXETER TRAMWAYS SYSTEM, APRIL 1929

Track	Almost five miles, just under half as single track, just over half as double
Tramcars	Twenty-eight, working at an average speed of $6^{1}/_{2}$ miles per hour
Working expenses	16.35d. per passenger mile
Earnings	19.08d. per passenger mile
Average fare per mile	$1^{1}/_{2}d$.
Workmen's fare per mile	1d.
Net capital liability	£42,180

tramways manager to Sheffield Corporation, a town with hills easily as steep as Fore Street. By April 1929 his report was ready, and in May he discussed it with the Tramways Committee. His report gives a snapshot of the workings of the trams in their final phase.

The Fearnley Report made four key points:

**Track renewals are urgently required and will cost
£10,000 (£450,000 at modern-day prices)**
• Four areas of work need to be tackled in the near future. These are at the two ends of the Pinhoe Road to Alphington Road service, at the end of Paris Street near the depot, and the up-track in Fore Street.

Corrugated rails need attention and will cost £2,000
• The corrugation of the rails causes a considerable amount of noise, and this can only get worse.

Narrow streets are unsuitable for tramway operation
• By comparison with trams in eleven other cities, the Exeter average speed, at 6½ miles per hour, was the lowest. In London trams reached over 9½ miles per hour.
• In the High Street, the maximum width kerb to kerb is only 30ft 9in, the minimum is 22ft 9in, and in Fore Street the position is even worse.
• Motor traffic will increase every year, and the position will get worse.

The proposed extension to Whipton cannot be justified
• The three-quarters of a mile extension proposed would cost about £21,000

Fearnley's conclusion was that trams should be superseded by buses and during the run-up to change no extension should take place and no track should be replaced. He advised the committee that motor buses were more suitable than trolley buses and that the modern bus was capable of tackling Exeter's hills. The committee went ahead to inspect suitable low-platformed double-deckers, but they were not convinced by Mr Fearnley's arguments, considering that some of the points had been overplayed. In July 1929 they decided that they should recommend to the council that the trams should continue for a further five years, and that an extension should be funded, although only down the Pinhoe Road to Polsloe Bridge, not as far as the city boundary.

Meanwhile the chief constable, who reported not to the Tramways Committee but to the Watch Committee, and who was the corporation's own traffic expert, had been preparing a report to the Watch Committee on High Street congestion. He had undertaken his own snapshot survey on 31 December 1928, from which he concluded that foremost amongst the difficulties, which included stationary vehicles, horse-drawn vehicles moving at a slow pace and inadequate footpaths for the pedestrian traffic, were the trams. He noted in particular that at one stop, just below the Queen Street junction, in the peak hour between 12 noon and 1 p.m., twenty-seven trams stopped and the traffic was as a consequence held up for more than twenty-nine minutes. The fact that so much of the city centre was subject to single-track working, so that trams had constantly to wait for another tram to clear the section ahead before they could proceed, was one of the causes of delay. Another was the sheer number of stops. Between the top of the High Street and Alphington Street there were thirteen regular tram stops and a further six request stops. His report also compared trams with buses for safety and mobility, and concluded: 'I am decidedly of opinion that buses would be a considerable advantage over trams.'

The presentation of this report to the Watch Committee in September 1929 alarmed the advocates of trams. Although the council had still not arrived at a firm recommendation, the Labour Party decided to try to use the retention of the trams as a rallying call to encourage voters to support their candidates in the November elections for the council. The slogan read:

> 'SOS'
> The Trams are in Danger.
> They are yours. Don't let them take them away.
> The City Council are wobbling.
> They cannot make up their minds.
> Help us to compel them.

To no avail, as their opponents pointed out, as they lost rather than gained seats in the elections. The new council met on 3 December 1929 with the Tramways Committee's recommendations before them:

1 That the council decide to continue the existing tramway services for three years from 1 April 1930, before the expiration of which period the council can again consider the position.
2 That the Pinhoe Road tramway be at once extended as far as Hamlin Lane.

The council, however, determined that this was yet another stalling move, and that they could not postpone their decision for a further three years. They refused to sanction the extension and required the Tramways Committee to produce a firm recommendation. With the assistance of Mr Fearnley this was finally ready for the Tramways Committee meeting in July 1930. After the August recess, the council finally agreed that the tram service should cease as soon as practicable, to be superseded by double-decker buses.

The Switchover

In January 1931, the tram service ceased along Alphington Road, where the track was in a dreadful condition, and the Alphington Road spur was served by buses to and from Exe Bridge. The Exeter Transport Committee (as the Tramways Committee was now called) showed in the Annual Report for 1930/1 that the use of the trams was already in decline, partly as a result of this first reduction, which had affected the last quarter's running, and partly as a result of the development of better bus services from the suburbs.

EXETER TRANSPORT COMMITTEE ANNUAL REPORT, 1930/1		
Section	£s generated 1929/30	£s generated 1930/31
St David's	5,611	5,495
Pinhoe Road	17,568	11,852
Heavitree	21,076	19,791

On 19 August 1931 Exeter said goodbye to its trams. At three o'clock that afternoon the mayor, Alderman Warren, drove the last tramcar from the Guildhall up the High Street to Belmont Road. Then the sheriff took over on a return trip. The longest-serving motorman, Chief Driver and Instructor Arthur Nicholls, motorman on the first car in 1905, took the tram down Fore Street to Exe Bridge. Councillors Hooper and Chick, who had been previous chairs of the Tramways Committee, took the tram out on a run to Heavitree. Then finally Mr E.C. Perry, who as chair of the Transport Committee and mayor in 1905 had driven the first tram, emerged from retirement to drive the last car from Heavitree down to the depot. Car no. 14, preceded by a pilot car full of civic dignitaries, had the honour of being the last tram of all.

92 (below left) *The mayor (Charles Warren) takes the controls of the last tram, car no. 14, as it sets out from the Guildhall on 19 August 1931.*

93 (below) *The chairman of the Transport Committee, H.E. Bradley, drives the tram along Cowick Street, with Motorman Nicholls behind him.*

94 *A large crowd had waited at the depot to bid their final farewells to the trams that had carried them so faithfully over the past twenty-six years.*

As they had done for the start of the electric tram service in 1905, the people of Exeter turned out in their hundreds to mark the occasion and to say goodbye. And, in order to signal the future, the tram was followed closely by a double-decker bus (see plate 95, *below*).

Afterwards there was a tea for the council and other dignitaries, and speeches. Councillor Bradley gave a summary of the success of the undertaking. Over its twenty-six years the trams had paid the city £22,190 in rates and the country £13,580 in taxes. After tea the mayor presented to Mr Perry the control handle of the last tram, silver-plated and suitably inscribed, and to Chairman Bradley the reverse lever, which also had been silver-plated and inscribed (see plate 21, p.34). Finally, it was the turn of Alderman John Stocker, who was the first vice-chairman of the Tramways Committee and had been a member of the

95 *E.C. Perry, who as mayor had driven the first tram, drove for part of the last journey. The mayor and sheriff are also on the platform.*

committee ever since, and who had bought the first tramways ticket issued in 1905, numbered 0001, for Mr Perry. Mr Stocker produced the very last ticket issued on the tramways account and gave this to Mr Bradley.

Last Words

The doom-mongers' prophecy that buses would not be able to take the load the trams had taken was not fulfilled. The buses were a success. The corporation noted in the first report from the Transport Committee (so renamed following the decision to switch over to a bus service) that the new service had been attracting greater numbers of passengers. Councillor Miss Splatt, who had supported the changeover, noted the 'gratifying' report and said, amidst council laughter, that she could not resist saying: 'I told you so!'

Did removing the trams ease the problems in the High Street? In the short-term perhaps, but by 1932 there were twenty-five vehicles a minute passing the *Express and Echo* offices in the High Street. The settings for the automatic signals at Exe Bridge could not cope at peak periods, and manual operation had to be used to ease congestion. Even the building of the new bypass along Hill Barton Road down to Countess Wear provided only short-term respite, and the length of queues to get through Exeter in the summer again became notorious.

Pressure for parking places to assist greater control of parking on the main streets began to mount again. The Watch Committee began work in 1931 on schemes such as unilateral parking in Sidwell Street and Queen Street. By 1934, proposals for the acquisition of Bedford Circus Green were being vigorously opposed by Mr McGahey and many of those who had offices in those beautiful surroundings. Parking places in Southernhay were also being considered.

> Alderman Ross, the very same Ross who had implacably opposed trams in the High Street, now had a new complaint: 'It always strikes me with a thrill of horror', he said, 'when I see the enormous double-deck buses coming down through the High Street.'
> The High Street in Exeter was in a fearful state, and it was impossible for them to carry on their business in such circumstances. People rushed into shops, flurried, hurried and worried by crossing the road, or coming up the street with all the hustle and noise going on.

The Last Traces of the Trams

The depot on Paris Street continued in use for the buses until the building of the Paris Street bus station after the Second World War, after which it became redundant and was eventually demolished. The Streets Committee were charged with taking up the track and, in consultation with the Electricity Committee, taking down the overhead poles where these were not required for street lighting. This work went on gradually over a number of years, starting with the Heavitree sections. Even by 1935 it had not been completed in the High Street.

The rolling stock was gradually disposed of. The transport

96 (left) *The internal construction of the tram shed, shown to good effect whilst empty and awaiting demolition, is of as high a standard as its exterior (see plate 36, p.49).*

97 (below left) *Several of Exeter's old trams were bought by a local scrap dealer and cut down. They made cheap and useful storage units.*

manager reported one month after the closure of the tram service that thirteen of the trams had already been disposed of, and there were thirteen to go. These went in response to advertisements for the best bidder. Some of them ended up in Plymouth, some in Halifax. Others went into quarry workings. A local scrap merchant dealer bought up the oldest cars and sold some on as storage units. At the end of the twentieth century a couple of cars were snapped decaying quietly in a field at Upton Pyne (see plate 97, *above left*).

98 (above right) *One of Exeter's trams found some years ago decaying quietly in a field at the village of Upton Pyne six miles up the Exe Valley.*

99 *The last working Exeter tram. Car no. 19, although reduced from a double-decker to a single-decker, still occasionally runs between Seaton and Colyton for Seaton Tramway.*

Nowadays the only remaining Exeter tramcar in service is on the restored tramway line at Seaton, operated by Seaton Tramway. This has been cut down from a double-decker to a single-decker but is still car no. 19 and, as the destination board in the photograph shows (see plate 99, *above*), still capable of transporting passengers – at least in their imaginations – to St David's station.

Sources for the Illustrations

Plates 1–9, 17, 66, 92–95 are from the Etched on Devon's Memory collection held by the Westcountry Studies Library.

Plates 10–12, 15, 16, 18, 22, 24–27, 30, 33–35, 37–40, 44–46, 49, 51–53, 58, 60, 63, 67–71, 74, 75, 77, 79, 81, 83–88 and 90 are from John Perkin's personal collection.

Plate 13 is from the Exeter Corporation Archive held by Devon Record Office.

Plates 14, 72, 73 and 82 were supplied by Dick Passmore.

Plates 19 and 20 were supplied by Sadru Bhanji.

Plates 23 and 99 were taken from the collection of Seaton Tramway.

Plates 28, 47, 54, 55, 56 and 62 and the photographs on pages 67 and 68 were taken from photographs lent by David Baker, Margaret Batten, Frank Potter and Pat Vaughan.

Plates 29 and 91 were supplied by Exeter Memories.

Plates, 31, 41, 42, 43 and 50 are from the collection held by the National Tramways Museum, Crich.

Plates 36, 64, 96, 97 and 98 are from a collection of photographs taken by Alan H. Mazonowicz.

Plates 57, 61, 78 and 80 were taken for this publication by Peter Caspar.

Plate 76 is from the collection of the South Western Electrical History Society.

Figures 1 and 2 were redrawn for this publication by Terry Russell, website at http://www.terryrusselltrams.co.uk/trthome.htm.

Cover Pictures

Front Cover. The cover of an ornamental box donated to the mayor and corporation of the City of Exeter by E. Waller, consulting engineer, to commemorate the introduction of the electric tramways in 1905. The photograph was taken for this publication by David Cornforth.

Rear Cover: The painting of a tram at the Dunsford Hill terminus on Cowick Street has been donated by Sylvia Harding to the Civic Society.

Further Information and Reading

Exeter Memories. Website at http://www.exetermemories.co.uk

Folkes, John and Margaret (2005), *Exeter Postcards*, Tempus Publishing

Gentry, P.W. (1960), *The Tramways of the West of England*, The Light Railway Transport League

Harvey, Hazel (1986), *Discovering Exeter: Sidwell Street*, Exeter Civic Society

Newton, Robert (1968), *Victorian Exeter*, Leicester University Press

Passmore, Dick (2008), *Power to the City*, Little Silver Publications

Perkin, J.B. (1994), *Exeter and Taunton Tramways*, Middleton Press

Sambourne, R.C. (1976), *Exeter: A Century of Public Transport*, Glasney Press

South Western Electricity Historical Society website at http://www.swehs.co.uk/docs/piclist.html

Tarry, Frederick T. (1936), *The Police as a Career: A Handbook for Candidates and Constables*, A. Wheaton & Co.

Thomas, Peter (2007), *A Century of Exeter: Events, People and Places Over the 20th Century*, History Press

Turner, Keith (1996), *The Directory of British Tramways: Southern England*, Tempus Publishing

WHOTT (West Country Historic Omnibus and Transport Trust) (2005), *Exeter's Trams: A Celebration of the Centenary of Exeter's Electric Trams* (WHOTT website is at http://www.busmuseum/org.uk)

For other Exeter Civic Society publications see http://www.exetercivicsociety.org.uk

Index